THE
FIRST EPISTLE
OF PETER

THE
FIRST
EPISTLE OF
PETER

C. E. B. CRANFIELD

SCM PRESS LTD
56 BLOOMSBURY STREET LONDON WC1

To my
Father and Mother

First published January 1950

Printed in Great Britain by
Northumberland Press Limited
Gateshead on Tyne

CONTENTS

PREFACE

THE preface to so modest a work seems hardly the place to record my thanks to those distinguished scholars to whom I owe more than I can say; but some debts incurred in the actual preparation of this book must be mentioned. I gladly acknowledge my great indebtedness to the commentaries on 1 Peter, particularly to the excellent recent commentaries by Dr. E. G. Selwyn and Dr. F. W. Beare, and to the great theological dictionary to the New Testament edited by Dr. G. Kittel which I have frequently consulted. My thanks are also due to my friends, the Revs. C. K. Barrett and K. Grayston, the former of whom very kindly read the whole typescript with great care and the latter some parts of it. Their valuable comments and criticisms have enabled me to make a number of improvements—though I have not always acted upon their suggestions and am alone responsible for the blemishes which remain. My thanks are also due to the Delegates of the Oxford University Press for generously granting permission to reprint the Revised Version text of the Epistle, the whole of which appears consecutively, printed in small capitals; to Dr. Hugh Martin for much kindness and unfailing patience; and to my father for invaluable help with the proofs and the index. I should also like to mention an Epworth Press booklet on 1 Peter by the Rev. C. R. B. Shapland, which I have not seen since I lost my copy in the Mediterranean in 1942, but which was one of the things that first stimulated me to preach sermons on the Epistle.

The abbreviation LXX, which might puzzle some readers, stands for the Septuagint Greek Version of the Old Testament.

C. E. B. CRANFIELD

Cleethorpes, Lincs.
October 1949.

CHAPTER ONE

WRITER AND READERS
(1.1-2)

THE opening sentence of an ancient Greek or Latin letter followed a customary form: first the writer's name, then the recipient's, and finally a greeting. At its simplest it was just 'A to B greetings'; but in 1 Peter, as in other New Testament letters, each of the three parts is expanded and given a distinctively Christian significance.

The Writer

Some scholars (among them F. W. Beare,[1] one of the most recent commentators on this Epistle) have argued that PETER is a pseudonym and that the Apostle Peter cannot have been the author. But, while it is perfectly true that spiritual authority does not depend on literary authenticity and Beare is doubtless correct in saying that pseudonymity was 'an accepted and harmless literary device' involving no dishonest intention (so that there is nothing inherently shocking or disturbing in the suggestion that a later writer put his message into the mouth of St. Peter for the sake of dramatic effect), the actual arguments against the traditional authorship are not nearly as strong as has been made out.

For anyone reading the letter in the original language the most obvious difficulties in the way of accepting the Petrine authorship are the good Greek style and the extensive literary vocabulary. Is it likely, it is asked, that a Galilean fisherman, who at the beginning of the Apostolic mission could be described as 'unlearned and ignorant' (Acts 4.13) and for whom Greek was a foreign tongue, would ever have written some of the best Greek in the New Testament? But this difficulty disappears at once, if we attribute to Silvanus (mentioned in 5.12 as Peter's amanuensis) a rather more

[1] F. W. Beare: *The First Epistle of Peter*, Blackwell, 1947.

responsible share in the composition of the letter than that of a mere scribe writing to dictation. It is reasonable to attribute to him the refinements of Greek grammar and style and the literary vocabulary, while at the same time recognizing in the letter the message, personality and apostolic authority of Peter. This would also explain something else that would be surprising in Peter himself—the close familiarity with the Greek version of the Old Testament (the LXX), which the letter displays.

Another argument is based on the presence of so many apparent echoes of St. Paul. Is it likely, it is asked, that one leading Apostle would be so dependent on another? The two Apostles were not working in very close association at any rate during that part of their ministries for which we have information in the New Testament, and St. Paul's letters would hardly have become generally available outside the churches to which they were actually addressed until some time after his death. But what at first sight appear to be echoes of the Pauline epistles are accounted for partly by Silvanus' share in the writing of this letter, Silvanus having been already associated with the writing of two of Paul's letters (1 Thess. 1.1, 2 Thess. 1.1), and partly by the existence of a widespread common stock of catechetical material[1] (i.e. material for the instruction of converts) known alike to St. Paul, St. Peter, and their readers, and to which they appealed as to something already familiar and accepted.

Then again it is urged that 4.16 implies that to profess Christianity was in itself already a crime, whereas it is thought that this was not so until the time of the younger Pliny's correspondence with the Emperor Trajan (i.e. A.D. 111-112). But it is pressing the language of 4.16 much too far, to read into it the distinction between condemnation 'for the Name' and condemnation 'for crimes associated with the Name'. To the Christians themselves it can hardly have seemed a particularly important distinction, whether they were actually condemned on a trumped-up charge of incendiarism or for not worshipping the Emperor or simply for being Christians; from their point of view, whatever the

[1] For the evidence for this see E. G. Selwyn, *The First Epistle of St. Peter*, Macmillan, 1946, pp. 363ff.

legal complications may have been, Christians suffered because they were Christians.

Other objections to the Petrine authorship are the alleged lack of personal reminiscences of Jesus and also the meagreness of references to the Holy Spirit, which Beare thinks makes it impossible to believe that our letter was written by a leader of the Church in the Apostolic Age. The former objection is largely a matter of individual impressions; for others are struck by the number of touches that suggest to them an eye-witness and of reminiscences of sayings of our Lord. The latter objection, though impressive at first sight, loses much of its force, when we turn up the word 'spirit' in the concordance and notice how rarely it occurs in some Pauline epistles.[1]

One other argument may be mentioned—the contention that the Epistle contains references to the ideas and practices of the Hellenistic mystery-cults so numerous as to suggest that the author was a gentile, whose religious background was formed by the mysteries rather than by Judaism, and that the letter must have been written at a time when the mysteries had already shown themselves to be the main rival to Christianity, and therefore some time after the death of Peter. But the alleged traces of the mystery terminology are highly problematic, and it is doubtful whether any ideas or terms occur which cannot equally well be traced to other sources. If there are references to the mysteries in the letter, that does not by any means rule out the Petrine authorship; for there would be nothing surprising in Peter referring to them in a letter to largely gentile churches.

The position then seems to be that, provided we allow for Silvanus having been rather more than a mere amanuensis, there is no sufficient reason for denying the traditional authorship of 1 Peter. On the other hand, there are a number of considerations that support it, such as the interesting points of contact with the speeches[2] of Peter in Acts and

[1] Phil. four times, Col. twice, 1 Thess. three times, 2 Thess. three times: of these at least five do not refer to the Holy Spirit.

[2] It is not suggested that these are Peter's actual words, but they do represent at least what Luke thought appropriate, and perhaps contain primitive material from an Aramaic source. Cf. Selwyn, op. cit., pp. 33ff.

with the Marcan Passion narrative (a reliable tradition connects St. Mark's Gospel with Peter) and also a number of passages, which either suggest an eye-witness or have an additional significance and poignancy, if they come from Peter.[1]

We shall be on safe ground, then, if we conclude that the letter before us bears the apostolic testimony and authority of Peter, but that the style and expression are to a large extent due to Silvanus; that the date was A.D. 63 or early in 64 (before the outbreak in August of the Neronian persecution, in which most probably the Apostle lost his life); and that the place of writing was Rome. James, the Lord's brother, had been martyred in Jerusalem in 62. Some think that Paul also had already won the martyr's crown. It was a turning-point in the relations of the Church with the Roman Empire. Previously trouble had come mostly from Jewish animosity, while the imperial authorities had on the whole been a source of protection. The Church had been treated as a sect of Judaism, and therefore had shared the privileges allowed to Jews, particularly that of exemption from the obligation to sacrifice to the Emperor. The martyrdom of James by the Jewish authorities indicated forcibly the fact that Church and Synagogue were two distinct things, which anyway was becoming increasingly apparent as more and more gentiles entered the Church. It was clear that, when once the Roman authorities took account of this, the Christian community would be in a perilous plight. The leaders of the Church must have realized that a storm was gathering. That popular hostility was already strong is indicated by Nero's choice of the Christians as a scapegoat in August 64.

In this situation, when for the Christian community in Rome the air was heavy with forebodings of the approaching storm, Peter, who himself as an acknowledged leader of the Church could expect to be one of the first victims when the storm should break, decides that a message of encouragement must be sent to certain churches in Asia Minor, for which he apparently feels some measure of personal responsibility. We can imagine him talking the matter over

[1] e.g. 1.8, 2.20-25, 5.1-4.

with Silvanus, who seems to have been a kindred spirit as well as a trusted brother (5.12). The letter is to be sent in Peter's name, they decide, because his apostolic authority will naturally carry great weight; but, as Silvanus is a good hand at writing letters—he had helped to draft the important message of the Apostolic Council of Jerusalem (Acts 15.22f.) and had also been associated with Paul in the writing of 1 and 2 Thess.—the task of drafting the letter falls to him. Some readers have felt that 1.3-4.11 is in itself a unity and reads rather like a baptismal sermon. Perhaps it is a not unlikely suggestion that behind it lies a sermon preached by Peter at the previous Easter celebrations, when the catechumens were baptized. We can imagine Silvanus suggesting to him (as others have been known to do to modern preachers) that really that sermon he preached last Easter ought to be known to a wider circle than those who actually heard it—and, in fact, is just what is required for the present occasion! If something of the sort happened, then 1.3-4.11 would represent more or less what Silvanus could remember[1] of Peter's sermon transmuted into more elegant Greek than that of which the Apostle is likely to have been master. Peter would probably alter it a little, when his friend read it to him. Or maybe they composed it together, the little touches that suggest an eye-witness of Christ being due to the Apostle, the smooth style and classical words to the more educated scribe. The latter part would anyway be specially composed for the particular purpose of the letter, 4.12-19 referring more directly to the gathering storm and the apprehensions of the recipients.

After Peter's name there follows the description, AN APOSTLE OF JESUS CHRIST. The New Testament use of *apostolos* (a substantive formed from the verb *apostello*, ' to send ') derives, not from the use of the word in classical Greek, in which it usually denotes the sending of a military or naval expedition or the actual force sent or a group of colonists, but from the Jewish use of *shaliach* (from the root *shalach*, the Hebrew equivalent of *apostello*). This word denotes an authorized agent or representative. The

[1] Or had Silvanus a written text of it? If he had, that might account for his not bringing the vague reference to persecution in 3.14ff. into line with the situation reflected in 4.12ff.

word is expressive of function rather than status. The agent was appointed to carry out a particular mission; when it was once accomplished, the appointment lapsed. He was responsible to his principal; his was a derived and dependent authority. In so far as an agent was loyally carrying out his commission, it could be said of him that 'a man's agent is as himself' (cf. Matt. 10.40). But there is evidence that Jewish custom did not allow an agent to pass on his authority (cf. T. W. Manson: *The Church's Ministry*, 36f.).

The general agreement between the idea of *apostolos* in the New Testament and the idea of *shaliach* is clear (e.g. John 13.16, Matt. 10.40, 2 Cor. 8.23). It is also extremely probable that Jesus Himself used *shelicha*, the Aramaic equivalent of *shaliach*, of the Twelve. In the Gospels we hear of Him commissioning them as His agents to undertake a definite mission in His name (Mark 3.13ff., Matt. 10.5ff., esp. 40, Mark 6.7-13, 30, etc.). But at His arrest they all forsook Him and fled, and the commission had to be confirmed after the Resurrection (Matt. 28.16ff.). Henceforward the essential qualifications of an Apostle in the strict sense in the New Testament are: to have been a witness of Christ's resurrection and to have received a personal commission from the risen Christ. The authority of the Apostles, then, is real and august and determinative for the life of the Church. At the same time it is a derived and dependent authority. When Christ gave authority to His Apostles, He did not give up His own authority. They are responsible to their Lord. The flock is not handed over to Peter, but remains Christ's—'*my* lambs', '*my* sheep' (John 21.15ff.). John 13.16 seems to be a warning against any presumption on the part of the Apostles, any usurping of the rights of Christ. So here in our letter the word 'apostle' is essentially an exceedingly humble word; for it directs attention away from the Apostle's person to Him, whose Apostle he is, from the one sent to the One that has sent him. It serves to make it absolutely clear right from the start that the letter is about *Jesus Christ* and is written in His name and under His authority. Peter claims the attention of his readers, not on the ground of his own personal worth, as being better or wiser than they, but simply

because he must bear witness to Him whose commission he
has received.

The Recipients

The title added to Peter's name has already indicated that
this is no ordinary letter. The beginning of the second part
of the opening sentence—TO THE ELECT—makes it clear that
there is also something very special about those to whom it
is addressed. But just as the word 'apostle' focused attention, not on the person of the Apostle, but on Him, whose
Apostle he was, so it is with the word 'elect'. It does not
refer to anything special that the recipients were in themselves or that they had done, but to something special that
had been done to them. They were, as a matter of fact,
very ordinary people, belonging for the most part to the
lower strata of society. The special thing about them was
that they were the objects of God's choice or election. Both
the word and the idea derive from the Old Testament. God
had chosen Israel from among the peoples to be His special
people, not because of any desert or attractiveness on their
part, but because He loved them with a love that was undeserved, that had its ground not in them but in Him. Very
often Israel had misunderstood what God's choice implied.
They had thought of it too often merely as a privilege, without realizing the obligations it entailed. Sometimes they
had taken it for granted as something natural and necessary,
like the relation of a heathen god to his people, and forgotten
that it was the free choice of God's grace. But there had
not been wanting prophets to remind them of its real significance. With this word 'elect' Peter reminds his readers
that, gentiles though many of them are, they too belong
now to the people of God, they have entered upon the inheritance of Israel and have a share both in its glorious
privileges and in its obligations. 'Elect' is a theme-word
of the Epistle (cf. 2.4, 6, 9, 5.13).

WHO ARE SOJOURNERS OF THE DISPERSION. . . . 'The
Dispersion' had come to be a technical term to denote the
Jews who were living outside Palestine. Some have thought
that it is the Jewish Dispersion that is meant here and that
therefore the people addressed must have been Jewish Chris-

tians; but there are several things in the letter, which seem
to indicate that there were gentiles among the recipients (see
1.18, 2.10, 4.3, and the passage devoted to slaves—not many
Jews were slaves). In fact, it is much more probable that
the people addressed would be mostly gentiles and that we
have here one more example of that taking over by the
Church of the names and titles of Israel. As the Church is
the new Israel, so also it is a new Dispersion. There was a
twofold reference in the use of the word. On the one hand,
it denoted the fact of being scattered; on the other, it reminded the Jews abroad of the homeland and the metropolis and the Temple, the centre of their life even though
they were far away. Similarly, when the word is applied
to the Church—the Christians, to whom Peter writes, are
scattered and dispersed in a hostile world as aliens; but they
have a home-country and a metropolis, for their ' citizenship
is in heaven' (Phil. 3.20).

Some of them were to be found IN PONTUS, GALATIA,
CAPPADOCIA, ASIA AND BITHYNIA, five districts, which together
included, roughly speaking, the whole of Asia Minor north
of the Taurus Mountains, an area with a fascinating and
varied history and—in the first century A.D.—a mixed population made up of Phrygians, Greeks, Celts, Persians and
Jews, in addition to the indigenous Anatolian stock. Asia
(i.e. the Roman province of that name, which comprised the
western end of Asia Minor) was one of the wealthiest and
most thickly populated parts of the Empire. It was rich in
great and ancient cities, where trade and culture flourished.
The cities were as Greek as any in Greece itself, though
there was a less Hellenized hinterland. Asia—or at least a
part of it—had been a Roman province since 133 B.C.
Pontus and Bithynia, which at this time formed a single
province, were also largely Hellenized. The cities were
thoroughly Greek, dating from the great days of Greek
colonization. Bithynia produced many eminent men of
letters. The other two districts were much less Greek in
culture. Cappadocia had only a few cities, though it
possessed an ancient civilization of its own. The native
language was still spoken in the first century B.C. It was a
wild, rugged country of dense forests and deep ravines, not
easily accessible. Galatia, which comprised most of the

central table-land of Asia Minor, was inhabited by a Celtic population, descendants of Gallic tribes that had established themselves in the heart of Asia Minor about 280 B.C. Greek was spoken in some of the towns, but the Celtic language still persisted. On the whole, the area was very prosperous and the general level of culture was high; but there were some big inequalities in the distribution of wealth, particularly in some parts, and of course everywhere a great proportion of the population were slaves. From the fact that the letter deals with the duties of Christian slaves (2.18ff.) but not with those of Christian masters we may guess that the majority of those addressed were slaves. But it should be remembered that slaves were often well-educated and refined.

The religious situation of Asia Minor was as varied as its racial make-up. There were the official rites and ceremonies of traditional Greek religion, but the Stoic and Epicurean philosophies on the one hand and the mystery-cults on the other were taken more seriously. There were also the various native cults, mostly of an orgiastic type and often immoral. The orgiastic kind of cult was especially characteristic of Phrygia (the eastern, inland part of the province of Asia). In addition there was the official worship of the Emperor, and there were temples to Augustus and high priests of his cult in the various districts who exercised civic as well as religious functions. The neglect of this official cult was punishable by law, though the Jews (here, as throughout the Empire) were exempt from this obligation, and so long as Christians were regarded as a branch of Judaism they too were in a privileged position. The earlier part of the letter gives no indication of official persecution by the authorities, but suggests rather an unofficial social persecution and social embarrassment and inconvenience; but 4.12-19 seems to hint at a more serious state of affairs. At any rate the position of Christians in Asia Minor, as elsewhere in the Empire, was very insecure, and many must have realized that trouble was on the way. It would seem that there was a good deal of apprehension among those to whom the letter was addressed, and that its purpose was to strengthen them in their loyalty and determination to stand firm and steadfast.

The first part of verse 2 sets forth in three sonorous phrases the meaning of their election—its origin, the manner of its being made effective, and its practical expression and purpose.

Very easily do we fall into the way of regarding only the human and visible aspect of the Church and thinking of it merely as a human organization. As far as the eye can see, there may very often be little to encourage us, whether we are first-century Christians in Asia Minor or twentieth-century Christians in Britain. If all our attention is concentrated on the hostility or indifference of the world or the exiguousness of our own progress in the Christian life, we may well be discouraged. At such times we need to be reminded that our election is ACCORDING TO THE FOREKNOW-LEDGE OF GOD THE FATHER. The Church is not just a human organization—though of course it is that. Its origin lies, not in the will of the flesh, in the idealism of men, in human aspirations and plans, but in the eternal purpose of God. It is God's people, chosen by Him 'before the foundation of the world' (Eph. 1.4; cf. 2 Tim. 1.9). Moreover, this is not only true of the Church as a whole; it is true also of each individual member. Severally as well as corporately they are 'elect . . . according to the foreknowledge of God the Father'. To remember this has always a steadying and strengthening effect. They might be only slaves, they might be brutally treated by cruel masters, they might themselves be only very poor Christians, their faith feeble, their victories but few. But they too may trace back the origin of their Christian status to God's eternal purpose. They are Christians because they are objects of God's gracious choice. Their lives are in His hands. They have a divinely appointed task to fulfil. The foreknowledge of God includes the distinct though closely related ideas of divine purpose, divine choice, divine providence, and carries with it the assurance that their high destiny shall be accomplished. Their existence now as Christians is part of God's will and purpose, embraced in the divine plan, and He, who has included their little lives in His eternal purpose and chosen them, is working together with them in all things for good, ruling and over-ruling in His providence (Rom. 8.28), to the end that His gracious purpose may be accomplished. Remembering the divine foreknowledge and all it implies, they must stand firm, having a sure and certain hope; for God's foreknowledge is the pledge of their salvation.

While their election has its origin in the purpose of God the Father, it is IN SANCTIFICATION OF THE SPIRIT, i.e. by the sanctifying activity of the Holy Spirit that it is being made effective. The word 'sanctification'[1] in the New Testament denotes the Christian's development effected by the Holy Spirit (with particular stress on the ethical side). Their faith in Christ is not the achievement of their own superior moral character or intellectual insight ('I believe,' says Luther, 'that I cannot by my own reason or strength believe in Jesus Christ my Lord or come to Him'), but rather a miracle wrought by the Holy Spirit (cf. 1 Cor. 12.3). To His sanctifying activity they owe the very fact that they believe; for He it was who in the first place made them open to the Gospel, as it were coming secretly and unloosing the latch from the inside, and restored to them the freedom to believe. And it is to Him they owe the preservation and increase of their faith. Their day-to-day existence is life in the Spirit, the field of His sanctifying activity.

The third phrase denotes the practical expression and purpose of their election. They are elect UNTO OBEDIENCE AND SPRINKLING OF THE BLOOD OF JESUS CHRIST. The phrase contains a reference to Exod. 24.7f., as is made clear by the association together of obedience and the sprinkling of the blood. Election involves duty and responsibility as well as privilege. It is election unto obedience. The sprinkling of the blood of Jesus Christ refers in the first place to the establishment of the new covenant between God and His people by the death of Christ, ratified by His blood. The new covenant rests on the forgiveness of sins (cf. Jer. 31.31 and 34c; Matt. 26.28: Jesus had Himself, it seems, associated together Exod. 24.7f., Jer. 31.31ff., and Isa. 53). Perhaps there is yet another idea present in this phrase—that of consecration; for the sprinkling of blood was also part of the ritual for the consecration of priests (Exod. 29.20-22,

[1] 'Sanctify' and 'sanctification' represent Greek words derived from the word that is translated 'holy' (sometimes 'saint'). In English the fact of this connection is obscured. For the meaning of 'holy' see further pp. 35ff.

B

Lev. 8.30). Compare the idea of the holy priesthood in 2.5, 9. The goal and the outward expression of the election of these Christians in Asia Minor—as of all Christians—is obedience to the Lord Jesus Christ. They must obey Christ, as those, with whom God has entered into a new covenant through His atoning death, who live in the strength of His forgiveness, and who have been consecrated by the sprinkling of Christ's blood to God's service. It is an obedience, which begins in this life, but is to be perfected in that other world, where sin will be finally purged away, when the saints have 'washed their robes, and made them white in the blood of the Lamb' (Rev. 7.14).

The Greeting

Now at last we come to the actual salutation—GRACE TO YOU AND PEACE BE MULTIPLIED. The ordinary Greek epistolary salutation was *chairein*—'greeting'—(used in the New Testament in Acts 15.23, 23.26, Jas. 1.1). For this is substituted the word *charis,* derived from the same root, a word that had become a technical term of the Gospel— 'grace', which signifies God's love in action in Jesus Christ on behalf of sinners. The ordinary Hebrew salutation on meeting and parting was 'peace' (*shalom*). Doubtless it was often used as a mere convention with little meaning; but in the Old Testament peace is often more or less the equivalent of 'salvation', and is used especially of the salvation or peace that will mark the days of the Messiah. (Cf. Isa. 9.6f., 52.7.) It is regarded as God's gift—e.g. Num. 6.26. The rabbis connected the greeting with this peace of the Messiah. Jesus had given it deep significance. On His lips it is not a mere pious wish, but His gift, which as Messiah He is able to bestow. See Mark 5.34, Luke 10.5f., John 14.27, 16.33, 20.19, 21, 26. John 16.33 especially throws light on the use of peace here as a greeting to those who face a perilous future. It was the characteristic Christian greeting, that Jesus and His first disciples had used, and that was used by the early Church, e.g. in the Liturgy. The eschatological[1]

[1] From 'eschatology', which means teaching about the Last Things.

meaning—peace of the Messiah, peace as equivalent of salvation—is in the New Testament fundamental. The other meanings, reconciliation between man and God, between man and man, and peace as peace of mind, are secondary to this basic meaning. What in an ordinary letter would be merely a convention is here filled with deep significance. It is a prayer that the recipients of the letter may know in ever-increasing fullness the grace and peace of God in Jesus Christ.

CHAPTER TWO

A LIVING HOPE

(1.3-12)

ONLY a few months and the Neronian persecution will have burst upon the Church in Rome, where the Apostle is writing, and have cost it many martyrs —among them the Apostle himself. Already the storm-clouds are gathering. There is an oppressive sense of insecurity. The Christians in Asia Minor, to whom this letter is addressed, are also seriously alarmed, and, we suspect, somewhat liable to give way to self-pity. The letter is written 'to confirm the feeble knees'. How does it begin? Not by offering sympathy, not by trying to convince them that what they fear will never happen, nor yet with a rehearsal of the writer's own troubles, but with an ascription of praise and thanks to God—BLESSED BE . . . The actual form of expression—' blessed be ' followed by the Name of God and a clause giving the particular ground for thanksgiving—was a characteristic feature of Jewish prayer.

But notice how St. Peter will not risk being misunderstood. The God, to whom he wants to ascribe praise and thanks, is the God who has revealed Himself in Jesus Christ, THE GOD AND FATHER OF OUR LORD JESUS CHRIST. He is not to be thought of apart from Jesus Christ. Peter is not attracted by those misty regions of religion-in-general, which have such a strong fascination for some modern Christians. He prefers to be specifically Christian. The words ' Jesus Christ ' occur four times in the first three verses.

So we are not surprised to find that the clause, which gives the ground for thanking God, is concerned with Christ. There are, of course, all sorts of things, for which we should be thankful to God; but perhaps one of the worst forms of ingratitude is to be so occupied with thanking God for His innumerable lesser mercies, that we forget to thank Him for His supreme Gift. St. Peter will run no risk of falling into this ingratitude. Where some of our minor hymn-writers would have indulged in a catalogue of the beauties of nature, he goes straight to the heart of the matter. God is to be blessed for what He has done for us in Jesus Christ.

When our minds are occupied with the Gospel, there can be no room for any thought of our merit. We can only acknowledge humbly and gratefully our immeasurable debt to God, WHO ACCORDING TO HIS GREAT MERCY has done for us what we could never do for ourselves and have not in the least deserved and can never repay.

To describe what God has done in Christ is far beyond the reach of human words; but, though the attempt must beggar language, it must nevertheless be made. So Peter resorts to metaphor. God BEGAT US AGAIN UNTO A LIVING HOPE. To beget is, at all events, a decisive act and the life that results is something new. So the metaphor at least points to the momentousness and newness of what has been accomplished.[1] At the same time it indicates that this radical transformation is altogether God's doing; for a child can hardly co-operate in its own begetting. Something utterly decisive has happened, an altogether new situation has been brought about. The Gospel is the good news: 'Behold I make all things new' (Rev. 21.5). And the turning-point, the decisive moment, was Christ's resurrection. It was BY THE RESURRECTION OF JESUS CHRIST FROM THE DEAD that God begat us again. When God raised Jesus Christ from the dead on the first Easter morning, He transformed the whole situation of mankind—and indeed of the whole universe. Christ's resurrection was the centre and heart of the Apostles' preaching (see especially Acts 1.22, 4.33). It was the secret of the note of triumph and certainty, which was so characteristic of the life and worship and evangelism of the early Church. We may well ask whether much of our present weakness and lack of

[1] For this metaphor cf. 1.23, 2.2, John 1.13, 3.1-15, James 1.18, 1 John 2.29, 3.9, 4.7, 5.1, 4, 18.

vitality is not connected with the fact that it is not so central with us.

We may, of course, distinguish two ' moments ' in God's begetting us again: that of Christ's resurrection on the first Easter morning, on the one hand, and on the other, that of a particular man's incorporation into Christ by the Holy Spirit, his being made a member or limb of Christ's body, a sharer in Christ's death and burial and resurrection. It is probable that Peter is thinking of Baptism,[1] in which the two ' moments ' are sacramentally one. As the outward seal and sign and symbol of a particular man's being made a sharer in Christ's death, burial and resurrection (cf. Rom. 6.3-11), Baptism is ' the sacrament of regeneration ', i.e. the outward seal and sign and symbol of his being begotten again by God.

The first Easter opened up a new world of unexpected beauty and splendour. Those early Christians were like someone who has climbed a mountain through cloud and driving rain and all the way up has had no view—and then suddenly, when he is at the summit, the cloud disperses and there is unveiled before him a wide and glorious expanse of country that he has never seen before. The most striking characteristic that distinguished the early Christians from their pagan neighbours was their *hope*. God had begotten them again ' unto a living hope '. When St. Paul described the pagan as ' having no hope ', it was no mere rhetorical flourish, but plain truth. The world of ancient Greek and Roman civilization was a world of fascinating beauty. It could boast of splendid courage, high intellectual power, and superb loveliness of poetry and art; but in spite of all the grandeur and charm it was a world without hope. Warmth there was in the enjoyment of the present, but the thought of the future struck chill. Old age was dreaded as the threshold leading out into the dark and cold. Life was a Damoclean banquet, sumptuous indeed but with the threatening sword all the time suspended by a thread. ' Not to be born at all—that is by far the best fortune; the second best is as soon as one is born with all speed to return thither whence one has come.' The words come from the greatest

---

[1] Cf. 3.21.

period of Greece, from fifth-century Athens, and from a man who was regarded by his contemporaries as an example of supreme good fortune, handsome, rich, of fine intellect, with public service as a military commander behind him, a superb poet, popular. They occur in a chorus of Sophocles, where the poet may be taken to be expressing his own thought. Over that classical civilization death reigned as king of terrors, spoiling men's enjoyment of the present with the intruding thought of the future, so that life could seem a gift not worth receiving, and death in infancy preferable to growing up to the conscious anticipation of having to die.

Now by the resurrection of Christ the king of terrors had been dethroned.

> '*Jesus lives! henceforth is death*
> *Entrance-gate to life immortal.*'

Unlike their pagan neighbours the early Christians were men of hope, who could look steadily into the future without fear, not with mere resignation, but with eager anticipation. A new dimension had been given to their lives—the dimension of the future, of eternal life.

At this point the New Testament puts to us a question that presses for an answer—Is this living hope as characteristic of us as it was of them? Do we really know what Peter is talking about? Do our lives in fact stand out from the dreary background of modern paganism with the same striking contrast as did those of the first Christians from the paganism of the first century? Or would it perhaps be more true to say that in our over-anxiety to be this-worldly and practical we are in grave danger of losing that very dimension of eternity that brought such new zest into their lives, and which alone can give zest to our practical concerns?

Hope is the theme of this whole section; though the actual word does not occur again, the idea runs through it like a golden thread and holds it together. Two other themes closely connected with hope occur and recur—' salvation ', the Christian's inheritance, the object hoped for, and ' joy ', the joy that accompanies the living hope. So the threads are woven into a pattern—' unto a living *hope* . . . unto an *inheritance* . . . unto a *salvation* . . wherein ye greatly *rejoice* . . . ye *rejoice* greatly with *joy* unspeakable and full of glory . . . the *salvation* of your souls . . . concerning which *salvation* . . .' It sparkles and shimmers with joyful expectancy; we might call it the paragraph of the broad panorama.

This new land stretched out before us is now further described as an inheritance. God has begotten us again UNTO AN INHERITANCE. It is a word rich in associations for those Christians who know the Old Testament; for again and again it is used there in connection with the land of Canaan—'the land which the Lord thy God giveth thee for an inheritance' (Deut. 15.4, 19.10), the promised land, which the aged Moses had seen stretched out before him, as he stood on the top of Pisgah and gazed with longing eyes westward and northward (Deut. 34). In every true Jewish heart the thought of that inheritance stirred emotions too deep for words. Yet that inheritance could not truly be described as INCORRUPTIBLE, AND UNDEFILED, AND THAT FADETH NOT AWAY. Too often had it been ravaged[1] by invading armies, Assyrians, Chaldeans, Greeks, Romans. Too often had it been defiled by Israel's own sins. Too often had its beauty faded, blasted by war or pest or drought, God's chastisements of His rebellious people. The inheritance, about which the Apostle is speaking, is a new Canaan, one that cannot be ravaged by hostile armies or defiled by sin, one whose beauty is fadeless.

What then is this incorruptible inheritance, this new Canaan? The Old Testament provides us with a further clue. There is another use of 'inheritance' in the Old Testament, that we have not mentioned. The Lord Himself is sometimes spoken of as the inheritance of the faithful. 'The Lord is the portion of mine inheritance' (Ps. 16.5, cf. 73.25f., Lam. 3.24). That new Canaan, that the resurrection of Christ lays open to our view, is fellowship with God undimmed by sin. Jesus Christ Himself is our future, our inheritance incorruptible, undefiled, unfading.

And this inheritance is RESERVED IN HEAVEN FOR YOU (cf. Col. 3.1-3, where 'the things that are above' means Jesus

[1] The Greek word translated 'incorruptible' is rich in suggestiveness. One of the meanings of the verb *phtheiro*, from which it is formed, is 'to ravage'—of an army laying waste the land.

Himself 'seated on the right hand of God'). Perhaps St. Peter had in mind our Lord's words recorded in Matt. 6.19f. (cf. Luke 12.33, 18.22). The inheritance is in heaven, eternal; it is not a part of this world, which passes away. And it is reserved, i.e. kept safe for you by God. It awaits you surely, laid up in His safe custody, beyond the ravages of decay. The Greek word translated 'reserved' suggests constant watchfulness. No harm can come to this inheritance. Whether it be the stake or the wild beasts in the arena or concentration camp or atom-bomb—these things can destroy our bodies, but they cannot touch our treasure. That is kept safe for us.

But, if God is keeping our inheritance safe for us, He is also keeping us safe for the enjoyment of our inheritance. That is the point of verse 5—WHO BY THE POWER OF GOD ARE GUARDED THROUGH FAITH UNTO A SALVATION. . . . 'Guarded' is a military term. As a garrison guards a city, so God's power guards the Christian. The same word is used in Phil. 4.7. And it is 'unto a salvation' that we are guarded. This is the real meaning of God's providence— not that we are to be exempt from the griefs and pains of this life, but that in and through all things He will bring us at the last to our salvation. It would be but a poor providence, if it shielded us from the troubles of this life and then were to fail to bring us to our inheritance in the end. It would be like bringing a ship safely through the perils of the high seas and then failing to navigate the river mouth.

'Salvation' is the word that denotes the whole sum of what God has in store for us, the enjoyment of our inheritance. The New Testament sometimes appears to speak of it as something of the present (e.g. Luke 19.9, 1 Cor. 15.2, 2 Cor. 2.15), sometimes as something that has already happened (e.g. Rom. 8.24, Eph. 2.5, 8, Tit. 3.5); but there are no occurrences of 'save', or 'salvation', which (when carefully considered) invalidate the statement that salvation in the New Testament is always regarded as something of the future—eschatological,[1] if you like the word. Past tenses are certainly sometimes used, because the decisive act of God, which secured our salvation, is in the past; and the

[1] For the meaning of ' eschatological ' see note on p. 18.

present tense is used to denote our present waiting and struggling, which have salvation as their goal; but the actual enjoyment of salvation is not in this world, but in the world to come. To identify our present experience as Christians with what the New Testament terms salvation is a disastrous illusion. Its result is that we lose sight of the infinite riches God has in store for us, 'which eye saw not, and ear heard not, and which entered not into the heart of man', and so we impoverish that very experience, the importance of which we were so anxious to magnify. Peter guards against any such illusion by describing salvation as READY TO BE REVEALED IN THE LAST TIME.

The hope, which is the theme of this whole section, looks to the future; but it means present joy. This is what verses 6-9 tell us. Reading the R.V. text, we might suppose that the antecedent of WHEREIN is 'salvation' in the previous verse; but that is impossible, since 'wherein' in the original must have either a masculine or neuter antecedent, and 'salvation' is feminine. So the antecedent might be 'God' or, just conceivably, 'the last time'. Much more probably it is the whole situation described in verses 3-5, and the sense is then 'Wherefore' or 'Seeing that this is so'. Because you hope for this salvation in the future, YE GREATLY REJOICE—now. The Christian life is a life of joy, a deep and full and abiding joy, that does not vanish at the approach of trouble. Ye greatly rejoice, Peter says, THOUGH NOW FOR A LITTLE WHILE, IF NEED BE, YE HAVE BEEN PUT TO GRIEF IN MANIFOLD TEMPTATIONS or trials. Here for the first time he mentions those trials, which, we may be quite sure, were very much in his readers' thoughts. He does not mention them, until he has first spoken of the heavenly inheritance and the present hope and joy. Only in this context can they be seen in true proportion. Against such a background the manifold temptations, however unpleasant, begin to look smaller. Compared with the promised inheritance they are only short-lived—only 'for a little while'. That is the point of the familiar words:

> 'Brief life is here our portion,
>   Brief sorrow, short-lived care;
> The life that knows no ending,

The tearless life is there.
O happy retribution!
Short toil; eternal rest. . . .'

Moreover, the trials of Christians are not meaningless. They serve a purpose, and that purpose is THAT THE PROOF OF YOUR FAITH (or 'the proved, i.e. the genuine, part of your faith', that which is left after what is false has been refined away, or perhaps, 'the sterling quality of your faith '), BEING MORE PRECIOUS THAN GOLD THAT PERISHETH THOUGH IT IS PROVED BY FIRE, MIGHT BE FOUND UNTO PRAISE AND GLORY AND HONOUR AT THE REVELATION OF JESUS CHRIST. Why, the very sharpness of the trials that test our faith is an evidence of its preciousness! A tried and tested faith, refined by sufferings and made mature, is far more precious than gold, which is transient in comparison. The process of refining is painful; but its purpose is that at the last we may receive praise and glory and honour.

And for those who love Jesus Christ, even though they have never seen Him, what could be more desirable than to have praise and glory and honour at His coming, WHOM NOT HAVING SEEN YE LOVE? There is perhaps an implied contrast in these words between the situation of the readers and that of the Apostle. They have not seen; but there are some who saw, and who can bear apostolic testimony to 'that which we have seen with our eyes, that which we beheld, and our hands handled'. And the writer is one of them who saw. Because they saw, and bear witness, it is possible for others, who have not seen, to believe. In this phrase, and still more in the following one, there would seem to be a reminiscence of the words of Jesus to Thomas, which Peter would have heard, 'Because thou hast seen me, thou hast believed: blessed are they that have not seen, and yet have believed' (John 20.29). ON WHOM, THOUGH NOW YE SEE HIM NOT, YET BELIEVING, YE REJOICE GREATLY WITH JOY UNSPEAKABLE AND FULL OF GLORY. The word 'now' implies a contrast with a 'then' that is not expressed, when the readers will see Him face to face (cf. 1 Cor. 13.12). The 'then' defies description. The 'now', in spite of sufferings, overflows with the joy of anticipation. That joy is already full of glory, lit up by the light of eternity.

Verse 9 drives home again the tension between present and future. RECEIVING is present, but its object, THE END (i.e. the issue or consummation) OF YOUR FAITH, EVEN THE SALVATION OF YOUR SOULS, is future. Already in the present you are receiving that which you will enjoy in the future. Perhaps St. Paul's illustration—or the illustration suggested by his language—in Rom. 13.12 helps as much as anything can to make this comprehensible. Down in the Alpine valley it is still dark, but those who will look up to the mountain peaks can already see the light of the new day and can live the remainder of the time of darkness in its strength and joy.

The last three verses of this section are concerned with the praises of this salvation. They adduce two facts to indicate its surpassing splendour: first that the Old Testament bears witness to it; secondly, that angels would fain catch a glimpse of it. It is possible that St. Peter has in mind the saying of Christ recorded in Luke 10.23f., Matt. 13.16f.: ' Blessed are the eyes which see the things that ye see: for I say unto you, that many prophets and kings desired to see the things which ye see, and saw them not; and to hear the things which ye hear, and heard them not.' He says: CONCERN-ING WHICH SALVATION THE PROPHETS SOUGHT AND SEARCHED DILIGENTLY, WHO PROPHESIED OF THE GRACE THAT SHOULD COME UNTO YOU (or ' the grace destined for you '). He is at one with the rest of the New Testament writers in his con-viction that the Old Testament is prophetic of Christ.[1] We need not limit ' prophets ' to the writings called generally by that name; the Law and the Writings were also regarded by the first Christians as prophetic—Psalms in particular were often appealed to. The men of the Old Testament had lived with their attention turned to the future, in expecta-tion of God's promised salvation of His people. Eagerly they scanned the far horizon, looking for the fulfilment of God's promises and their hopes, SEARCHING WHAT TIME OR WHAT MANNER OF TIME THE SPIRIT OF CHRIST WHICH WAS IN THEM DID POINT UNTO. . . . The Holy Spirit, ' Who spake by the prophets ', is ' the Spirit of Christ ' or Messiah; as later doctrine was to formulate it, He ' proceedeth from the

[1] Cf. Luke 24.25-27, John 5.39, 45-47, 8.56, Acts 7.52, 8.30ff., 17.2ff.; many other passages could be cited.

Father and the Son'. For the close connection between the Spirit and Christ we may compare John 14.26, 16.13f. (The tendency to separate the doctrine of the Spirit from the doctrine of the Person and Work of Christ has been a fruitful source of misunderstandings in the life of the Church.) The Spirit is regarded as having indicated the time of fulfilment, WHEN IT TESTIFIED BEFOREHAND THE SUFFERINGS OF CHRIST[1] AND THE GLORIES THAT SHOULD FOLLOW THEM.

The men of the Old Testament lived in the strength of God's promise, with their faces turned towards the future, knowing that the divine intervention, which they expected, could alone make sense of their life. In this sense they may be said to have lived by faith in Christ. Over their lives there stood a great 'not yet'. They knew that they were waiting for something which had not yet come. They were men, TO WHOM IT WAS REVEALED, THAT NOT UNTO THEM-SELVES, BUT UNTO YOU DID THEY MINISTER THESE THINGS, WHICH NOW HAVE BEEN ANNOUNCED UNTO YOU THROUGH THEM THAT PREACHED THE GOSPEL UNTO YOU. . . . They were still outside the kingdom (cf. Matt. 11.11). But, though only dimly discerning in the distance and not themselves enjoying, they were nevertheless truly ministering these things to us; for the forward-pointing of the Old Testament is an essential part of the foundation of our faith (cf. Eph. 2.20—prophets as well as Apostles). There is a real distinction between the Old Testament and the New, but also a no less real unity, and that unity—the fact that the forward-pointing fingers and the backward-pointing fingers are all alike focused on one Figure, Jesus Christ—is one of the most convincing evidences for the truth of the Gospel. Moreover, it is only against the background, and in the context, of the Old Testament that the apostolic proclamation can be rightly understood. The fact of the unity of the Bible is further underlined, when it is pointed out that those who

---

[1] Literally ' the sufferings unto Christ ', which is best understood to mean ' the sufferings destined for Christ '. Of particular passages in the Old Testament, which were taken to refer to the sufferings of Christ, the chief are Ps. 22 and Isa. 52.13-53.12. For the glories that should follow see especially Ps. 2 (Acts 13.33), Ps. 16.8-11 (Acts 13.35, 2.25ff.), Ps. 110 (Acts 2.34f., Heb. 7.17, 21, 5.6, etc.)

proclaim the Gospel do so by that same Spirit, who before witnessed in the prophets. Those, who proclaimed the Gospel to these Christians in Asia Minor, did so BY THE HOLY GHOST SENT FORTH FROM HEAVEN.

Now we come to that other fact that is adduced to show the surpassing splendour of the salvation we hope for— WHICH THINGS even ANGELS DESIRE TO LOOK INTO. It is possible that the writer has in mind the saying of Christ recorded in Luke 15.10, and that the point is that the angels are thrilled to look upon these things. But the word translated 'look', though it can mean simply 'to stoop down to look' (cf. Luke 24.12, John 20.11), often suggests a stolen glimpse, and it is probable that the meaning here is that the angels would fain peep into the blessedness of our salvation, but actually cannot do even that, because it is beyond their apprehension. If that is so, then Charles Wesley's words give the right sense—

> '*The first-born sons of light*
> *Desire in vain its depths to see,*
> *They cannot reach the mystery,*
> *The length, and breadth, and height.*'

We may compare also the children's hymn—

> '*A song which even angels*
> *Can never, never sing;*
> *They know not Christ as Saviour,*
> *But worship Him as King.*'

CHAPTER THREE

YE SHALL BE HOLY;
FOR I AM HOLY

(1.13-25)

So far we have heard a great deal about the future, about the inheritance reserved in heaven for us, the salvation ready to be revealed in the last time. The central theme of 1.3-12 was hope. It has been made clear that hope, joy, faith, and love to the unseen Master are marks of the Christian. But nothing has been said—at least directly—about what is sometimes called 'practical Christianity'. Does it mean that to be a Christian is simply to sit with folded arms and dream about the heavenly inheritance? Are we to be so preoccupied with thoughts of the future that we do nothing about the needs and possibilities of the present? If we have got that impression, then we have misunderstood the last section altogether. Verses 13-25 make that clear. They bring us—some of us perhaps with something of a bump!—to the present duties that follow from our living hope.

The first word—WHEREFORE—is thoroughly significant. What is now going to be said has a definite relation to what has just been said. It is to what he has just said that the writer appeals, as he goes on to exhortation—'Wherefore . . .' Because God has begotten you again to a living hope by the resurrection of Christ from the dead, because you have an incorruptible inheritance, a salvation ready to be revealed in the last time, *therefore* in the present you must be such and such. Compare the significant 'therefore' in Rom. 12.1. Christian ethics follow from divine grace.

What then has Peter to say about the practical implications of the Gospel, about the present obligations that follow from the Christian hope? The first thing he says will be rather a surprise for any who are inclined to belittle the place of the intellect in Christian discipleship. GIRDING UP

31

THE LOINS OF YOUR MIND—in the first place, get down to some hard thinking! Make a real effort to understand this hope of yours. Peter indulges in a quaint little joke, which is probably lost on most modern readers, who, being unfamiliar with the exigencies of ancient masculine dress and never having experienced the necessity of girding up their loins, do not form any vivid mental picture of what is said. In the ancient world men wore long robes. So, when they wanted to do anything at all energetic, they had to gather up their skirts under their belts. The modern equivalent of this girding up the loins is rolling up one's shirt-sleeves or at any rate taking off one's coat. We should get the same quaint incongruity that the writer intended if we were to render the Greek—'Rolling up the shirt-sleeves of your mind' or even 'taking off the coat of your mind'!

Such strenuous thinking, a necessity at all times in the Christian Church, can seldom have been more urgently needed than to-day. A time, when unparalleled technical means for the mass-production of ideas are close to the hands of the unscrupulous, is no time for Christians to be content with slipshod thinking and vague and hazy notions. It is a pathetic feature of contemporary Church life that there are still plenty in the pews who clamour for shorter and lighter sermons and bright and easy services and not a few in the pulpits prepared to pander to popular taste. There's a vicious circle: superficial congregations make superficial pastors, and superficial pastors make superficial congregations. Peter's slogan is a call to us to break the vicious circle, a call for sermons which teach, not merely entertain, and for Church members, who will not shirk the discipline of intellectual effort, a call to the strenuous but exhilarating adventure of trying to understand ever more and more deeply the Gospel, which surpasses all our understanding, and in its light to understand the problems of our day.

Closely connected with the need for intellectual effort is the need to BE SOBER. It is a word the Apostle likes; he uses it again in 4.7 and 5.8. It includes, of course, the avoidance of drunkenness; but that by no means exhausts its meaning. Positively, it denotes alertness and steadiness in thought and conduct; negatively, the refusal to allow our attention to be

distracted from our hope. We are to be balanced and steadfast, our eyes turned upward, as were those of Christian and
Faithful, as they passed through Vanity Fair, our feet
realistically on the ground. Biblical sobriety means resist-
ing alike the seductive distractions of this world, with which
we may so easily become intoxicated, and the stupid fanaticism of those who would make the Christian hope an excuse
for neglecting the plain duties of the present.

The third demand that our hope makes upon us is that we
should really hope! AND SET YOUR HOPE PERFECTLY ON THE
GRACE THAT IS TO BE BROUGHT UNTO YOU AT THE REVELATION
OF JESUS CHRIST. . . . Two things are vital here—that the
object of our hope be the right one and that we hope for it
unreservedly, wholeheartedly. We shall be on the wrong
track, if we understand this verse to mean that the grace
that is being brought to us is something quite separate from
the person of Jesus Christ who is going to be revealed.
Grace cannot be separated from Jesus Christ. Grace in the
New Testament means the redemptive action of God in
Christ, whether we are thinking of it in the phase of the
Incarnation or the Cross or the Resurrection or, as here,
in the final phase of the Consummation. So here what is
meant is that we are to set our hope without reserve on Him,
who 'shall come again with glory' as our Judge and Redeemer. That is something quite different from setting our
hope on some man-built Utopia. But those, whose hope
is most unreservedly concentrated on that grace, of which
our letter speaks, will, as a matter of fact, be the most
realistic and practical in their efforts here and now by con-
crete 'acts of obedience and faith' to set up on earth 'signs
which point to the coming victory' (message of the First
Assembly of the World Council of Churches, 1948).

Peter now moves on to a more detailed description of the
life demanded by the living hope. The thoughts refuse to
be confined in the trim strait-jacket of an orderly and meth-
odical arrangement, with the result that it is impossible to
make a neat analysis of what he is saying. We might compare these verses with a piece of weaving. The warp
describes the nature of the Christian life, while the woof
indicates its motives. The separate threads of the warp
characterize the Christian life as obedience to God (verse

14), holiness (15f.), the fear of God (17), and love of the brethren (22). The separate threads of the woof indicate the motives: first, God is holy and you belong to Him (15f.), secondly, you address the impartial Judge of all men by the intimate name of Father (17), thirdly, you have been redeemed by the precious blood of Christ (18-21), fourthly, you have been begotten again of the eternal Word of God (23).

The first thread of the warp describes the Christian life as a life of obedience to God—AS CHILDREN[1] OF OBEDIENCE . . . 'Obedience' is a key-word of the Epistle. Cf. 'elect unto obedience' in 1.2 and 'your obedience to the truth' in 1.22. The goodness, with which the New Testament is concerned, is not a matter of aspiration after a human ideal, but obedience to the divine imperative, not the attempt to measure up to human standards of behaviour, but submission to the claims of the living God. Obedience, like apostle, is a humble word. If we are preoccupied with our comfortable feelings and inclined to bask in the warmth of our religious experience, the word obedience here may be rather like an unexpected pail of cold water down our backs. Some of us do not like the sound of the word obedience or of the related word authority. We are naturally inclined to what Paul calls 'will-worship', wanting to feel free to serve God in ways of our own choosing instead of being content with the ways which He has commanded. For example, we may decide to stop away from Communion, because we do not feel that we get any good from it But God requires of us obedience to His commands, not help in recommending to Him what we think would be good for us!

For the first readers of this letter such obedience was going to involve a stiff struggle against the insidious attractions of the old lusts of their pagan past—NOT FASHIONING

---

[1] 'Children of obedience' could mean 'obedient children' (as A.V. renders it) the genitive being a genitive of quality, which is perfectly good Greek. But the idea of children would be rather abruptly introduced: the idea of Christians as God's children seems to be introduced as a new point in verse 17. So it is better to understand the phrase as a Semitism meaning simply 'obedient people'. Cf. 2 Sam. 7.10, Deut. 13.13, Mark 2.19, Luke 10.6, etc.

YOURSELVES[1] (better 'do not continue to fashion your-selves', the Greek participle being here equivalent to an imperative) ACCORDING TO YOUR FORMER LUSTS IN THE TIME OF YOUR IGNORANCE. The phrase 'in the time of your ignorance' suggests that the recipients were mostly gentiles. But for all of us there are elements in our lives that belong to a past that was buried with Christ, but has not been so completely left behind as it should have been.

The Christian life is next characterized as a life of holi-ness, and God's holiness indicated as its motive. BUT LIKE AS HE WHICH CALLED YOU IS HOLY, BE YE YOURSELVES ALSO HOLY IN ALL MANNER OF LIVING; BECAUSE IT IS WRITTEN, YE SHALL BE HOLY; FOR I AM HOLY (Lev. 11.44, 19.2, 20.7, 26) 'Holy' is another key-word. It will be worth our while taking some trouble to understand it. In the Old Testa-ment[2] its root meaning is 'marked off', 'separated', 'with-drawn from ordinary use'. In the surrounding heathenism holiness was conceived in a thoroughly naturalistic way. Certain places, objects, persons, were felt to be charged with a mysterious power which removed them from the sphere of the ordinary; there was a difference, an otherness, about them. This was regarded as communicable, rather like an infection that can be caught or an electric current that can be conducted. To approach or touch anything holy, unless one had been immunized (as a priest who was himself holy), was highly dangerous. The opposite to 'holy' was 'profane' or 'common', which denoted that which it was safe for an ordinary person to touch and use. In the heathenism surrounding Israel 'holy' was applied predom-inantly to objects, acts and persons, and only rarely to the actual deity; but in the Old Testament it is of Yahweh him-self that it is chiefly used, and the holiness of places, objects and persons is hardly ever understood in a merely imper-sonal, mechanical sense. It is this difference that radically distinguishes the Old Testament conception of holiness from the heathen. So, for instance, we misunderstand the holi-ness of the Ark, if we think of it simply as a ritual-object charged with an impersonal, material element or force; its holiness lay, rather, in its being the throne of the invisible

[1] For 'fashioning yourselves according to' cf. Rom. 12.2.

[2] Cf. W. Eichrodt, *Theologie des Alten Testaments*, I, 139ff.

King. Even 2 Sam. 6.6f., does not reflect the naturalistic idea of holiness (though at first sight it certainly seems to do so) for that which destroys Uzzah is not thought of as an explosion of an impersonal force with which the Ark is charged, but rather as a personal reaction on the part of Yahweh. This distinction is significant—though, of course, it is true that the passage does reflect a very primitive and imperfect knowledge of God. The uniqueness of the Old Testament conception of holiness lies not, as is often maintained, simply in its ethical content, but rather in the fact that holiness is not thought of in an impersonal, mechanical or naturalistic way, but as derived from the personal will of God and therefore involving an encounter with the personal demands of the living God, who claims the absolute allegiance of His people.

Under the prophetic influence the ethical element in ' the holy ' was emphasized; for, since holiness was derived from God's personal will, its significance was naturally governed by God's self-revelation as righteous, merciful, etc. But the ethical content never exhausted the meaning of ' the holy ', and the seriousness of the moral commandments derived, not from their intrinsic excellence, but from the holiness of the God who gave them. In the Holiness Code (Lev. 17.-26) ethical and ritual commandments stand together as the inviolable standards of men's intercourse with God. The holiness of the Lord denotes the absolute authority with which He confronts man.

But the word ' holy ' was also applied to Israel. The sentence quoted by Peter occurs more than once in the Holiness Code, and we may compare many other passages. The application of ' holy ' to Israel did not mean a blurring of the contrast between God and Israel, but rather that He had laid hold upon them to be His special people, set apart for His service. The contrast was still there; in fact, the holiness of the Holy One of Israel constituted a continual threat to their very existence, for it implied His judgment of their sins. The holiness of Israel derived from God's choice, but it involved the obligation on their part to be and to do what was in accordance with the character of the Lord their God. In other words, they were committed to the continual effort to express in their life the reality of their election by obeying God's laws and avoiding the defiling ways of the heathen. It involved such things as not keeping back a hired man's wages overnight, not reaping the corners of one's field or gathering the gleanings but leaving them 'for the poor and for the stranger', not stealing or dealing falsely, and not going up and down as a tale-bearer among the people. These and many like things were in the Holiness Code. It even included the thoughts and feelings: 'Thou shalt not hate thy brother in thine heart', 'Thou shalt love thy neighbour as thyself'.

Such was the Old Testament background of 1 Pet. 1.15f. The New Testament use of 'holy' rests squarely upon the Old Testament foundation. The holiness of God is presupposed everywhere in the New Testament. So too is the holiness of the new Israel, the Church, and of its individual members. They are saints (in Greek the same word as 'holy') by virtue of God's calling, but, as in the Old Testament the Israelite was to express this holiness in outward conduct, so in the New Testament the Christian is called to be 'holy in all manner of living'.

In verse 17 we come to a further characterization of the Christian life in the form of an exhortation. AND IF YE CALL ON HIM AS FATHER, WHO WITHOUT RESPECT OF PERSONS JUDGETH ACCORDING TO EACH MAN'S WORK, . . . You have been taught to address God as 'Father'. What follows from that? What conclusion are you to draw?—That you are thereby exempt from the obligation of obedience? On the contrary, what follows is that you must PASS THE TIME OF YOUR SOJOURNING (i.e. your life on earth) IN FEAR. It is of God's infinite condescension that you are allowed to call Him 'Father'. You are not to presume on His goodness, but rather let it make you reverent and humble. He has not ceased to be the impartial Judge of all men. The more truly, the more intimately, we know Him, the more of awe and reverence we shall feel. The 'fear of the Lord', which is 'the beginning of wisdom', includes the fear of His punishments (e.g. Matt. 10.28, Heb. 4.1, 10.31, 1 Tim. 5.20) —indeed, to cease to fear God's judgments is the climax of wickedness (Rom 3.18)—but it includes much more than this. In the Bible the love and the fear of God go together (e.g. Deut. 10.12, and cf. the words of the Litany, 'that it may please Thee to give us an heart to love and dread Thee . . .'). 'Fear' is another key-word in 1 Peter (cf. 2.17, 18, 3.2, 15, of the fear of God; in 3.6, 14 the fear referred to is a false fear). It is important to realize that the English word 'fear' has suffered change in the course of the years and its significance is more restricted in modern usage than in the seventeenth century. 'Reverence' would quite often be a closer modern equivalent.

But the truest and strongest motive for fear is the recollection of the cost of our redemption. The fear of God at its truest is inseparably bound up with the sense of gratitude, it is the fear of being disloyal to Him who died for us, of wasting the fruits of His death. The supreme motive for fear is the cross of Christ. KNOWING THAT YE WERE RE-DEEMED, NOT WITH CORRUPTIBLE THINGS, WITH SILVER OR GOLD, FROM YOUR VAIN MANNER OF LIFE HANDED DOWN FROM YOUR FATHERS; BUT WITH PRECIOUS BLOOD, AS OF A LAMB WITHOUT BLEMISH AND WITHOUT SPOT, EVEN THE BLOOD OF CHRIST. The key to the understanding of these two tremendously important verses is the word 'redeem'. What exactly does it mean?

'Ye were redeemed' represents the passive of the Greek verb formed from the noun *lytron*. In extra-biblical Greek both noun and verb have to do with the ransoming of prisoners of war, the manumission of slaves, and the redemption of pledges, the noun signifying in each case the price paid. *Lytron* is also used rarely of an offering given to a deity in expiation of wrong-doing. In the LXX the middle voice of this verb is used mainly to represent two Hebrew verbs, of which one denotes primarily the exercise of the next of kin's rights, whether in avenging blood, or, more often, in the redemption of alienated property or of kinsmen who have been enslaved, while the other denotes the redemption of the firstborn, and is also used of a man whose life is forfeit paying a ransom to redeem his own life. In the LXX, just as in extra-biblical Greek, *lytron* signifies the price paid. It is to be noted that in the redemption of the firstborn or in such an instance as Exod. 30.12 the *lytron* is thought of as being paid to God. Both the Hebrew verbs (and therefore also the Greek verb that represented them) came to be used metaphorically of deliverance from various distresses: e.g. from a lion, from death, from sin, above all of God's deliverance of Israel from Egyptian bondage and from the Exile. In these instances no ransom is paid and the meaning is simply 'deliver' or 'rescue'.

It is clear from what has just been said that if 'ye were redeemed' stood alone here in 1 Peter 1, it could be taken to mean simply 'you were delivered'; but this weakened sense, in which the idea of ransom is not present, is ruled out here by the reference to money, to the blood of Christ and to sacrifice, and also by the probability that the saying of Christ recorded in Mark 10.45 was in St. Peter's mind. In Mark 10.45 the noun *lytron* is used. Jesus interprets the meaning of His own approaching death by the words: 'to give his life a ransom for many'. The question arises: 'To whom then was the ransom paid?' We can at once rule out the suggestion that it was paid to the devil, there being no scriptural grounds for such a notion. The true answer is 'to God'. There is Old Testament precedent for the idea of the ransom paid to God, as we have seen; but the meaning of *lytron* in Mark 10.45 (and of the verb here in 1 Peter) is to be explained, not primarily by any *a priori* theology of sacrifice, etc., but rather in the light of the actual sufferings and death of Christ. The Gospels depict, not a calm, unflinching hero strong in the consciousness of his own innocence so much as One, who in face of death was 'sore troubled', not because He was less brave than other men, but because of the grim reality of His utter self-identification with us sinners. Mark 15.34 tells something of what it cost Him to offer up His life to His Father, a ransom for many.

In these two verses many strands of thought are intertwined and different ideas brought to the interpretation of the Cross: the thought of Israel's deliverance from Egypt by God's mighty intervention (as Israel had been delivered from bondage, so these Christians of Asia Minor had been delivered from their former vain manner of life, from the slavery of sin); the thought of sacrifice, particularly of the Paschal lamb (perhaps also the thought of the Suffering Servant of Isa. 53 likened to a lamb); the thought of redemption (the various uses of the verb formed from *lytron* in the

LXX). In addition to the thought of redemption as known in the Old Testament, the reference to silver and gold probably contains also a reference to the manumission of slaves among the gentiles. A slave could save up his hard-won earnings and at last, if he were lucky, buy his own freedom; this was doubtless something some of Peter's readers had done or hoped to do. But there was that other slavery, from which none could ever hope to buy his own release; not even a whole life's savings could pay the price of sin. Nothing less than Christ's death could do that. And those, who know themselves redeemed at such a cost—how can they help but have in their hearts a holy fear, lest by their sloth or wilfulness they should prove ungrateful?

We have heard about the cost of our redemption and that it is redemption from the slavery of sin. Peter now goes on to tell us of our redemption's 'transcendent origin' (Selwyn's phrase). There was nothing haphazard about Christ's death. It was in God's eternal purpose—WHO WAS FOREKNOWN INDEED BEFORE THE FOUNDATION OF THE WORLD (cf. Acts 2.23, and the 'must' of Mark 8.31, etc.). BUT He, whose work of redemption was purposed by God 'ere the worlds began to be', WAS MANIFESTED. . . . There came a time, when the Word, who in the beginning was with God, and by whom all things were made, at last became flesh, so that men might hear, and see with their eyes, and their hands handle, and those that received Him might behold His glory. That manifestation was AT THE END OF THE TIMES; for His coming constituted 'the fulness of the time', introduced the 'last days'. Since then men have been living in the last days. The final stage of history began with the Birth in Bethlehem (cf. Acts 2.16f., Heb. 1.2, 9.26, etc.), though it has yet to be consummated.

With the words FOR YOUR SAKE the writer 'focuses the whole divine counsel of redemption upon his readers' (Selwyn). The Gospel is absolutely personal. This is most clearly expressed in the sacrament of Baptism, which seems never to be far from the writer's mind in this letter. Compare the first person singular in Gal. 2.20 or in Watts' hymn, 'When I survey'.

The readers are further described as those, WHO THROUGH HIM ARE BELIEVERS IN GOD. It is through Jesus Christ—the

Way to the Father—that they have been enabled to know the living God and to trust in Him. But the word rendered ' believers ' is not the participle, as one might have expected, but the verbal adjective, which usually has the meaning ' loyal '. Probably the double meaning is intended: through Christ we believe, and also through Him we are kept loyal to God.

The further point, that God has sealed Christ's work as successful and certified to us the reality of our redemption by His resurrection, is here added (in accordance with the letter's very rich style)—WHICH RAISED HIM FROM THE DEAD, AND GAVE HIM GLORY; and the whole passage on redemption (18-21) is summed up by the declaration about the fruits of redemption in the life of the redeemed. You have been redeemed . . . SO THAT YOUR FAITH AND HOPE now, while you are still waiting for your heavenly inheritance, MIGHT BE IN GOD.

The Christian life is now finally characterized as a life of brotherly love. SEEING YE HAVE PURIFIED YOUR SOULS IN YOUR OBEDIENCE TO THE TRUTH—there is probably a reference to Baptism here; for the perfect participle (literally ' having purified ') suggests a definite act that has been accomplished. You have submitted to the truth of the Gospel, allowing yourselves to be baptized, and thereby you have been cleansed. The end in view was a new life; it was UNTO UNFEIGNED LOVE OF THE BRETHREN, for it meant your entry into the community of Christ's Church. Notice the connection between ' the truth ' and ' unfeigned '. The Gospel, to which you have responded, is God's truth, and any pretence of love would be quite out of keeping with ' the truth '. So you must LOVE ONE ANOTHER FROM THE HEART FERVENTLY. Live out the implications of your Baptism! (For ' fervently ' cf. p. 95.)

Here then is the practical, matter of fact, test of the reality of our Christian life—Do we love the brethren? There is no escape from this test. If we do not love the brethren, then all our talk about obedience, holiness, fear of God, is so much humbug (cf. 1 John 4.20f.). The words ' unfeigned ' and ' from the heart ' warn against all attempts to by-pass this test or slither over it. The love that is required is real love, love that acts, not any ' sentimental

professions which often do duty for brotherly love'
(Selwyn).

Verse 23 repeats in different words and from a different
angle what has already been said in the first half of 22.
The Word of God, which you have heard and to which
you have responded, is the means by which you have been
born again; and the origin of this new birth is not an act
of human contriving but an act of God—HAVING BEEN BE-
GOTTEN AGAIN, NOT OF[1] CORRUPTIBLE SEED, BUT OF INCOR-
RUPTIBLE, THROUGH THE WORD OF GOD, WHICH LIVETH AND
ABIDETH (cf. John 1.13).

In 24 and 25 we have a quotation from Isa. 40.6, 8, by
way of illustration and confirmation of the phrase 'the
word of God, which liveth and abideth': FOR,

ALL FLESH IS AS GRASS,
AND ALL THE GLORY THEREOF AS THE FLOWER OF GRASS.
THE GRASS WITHERETH, AND THE FLOWER FALLETH:
BUT THE WORD OF THE LORD ABIDETH FOR EVER.

In contrast with the transience of human life and all things
human, God's Word is eternal. AND THIS Word of God,
about which the prophet speaks, IS the same as THE WORD
OF GOOD TIDINGS WHICH WAS PREACHED UNTO YOU—the
message of the Good News of Jesus Christ.

---

[1] The Greek preposition *ek*, here rendered 'of', denotes the
source; the preposition *dia*, here rendered 'through', denotes the
means or instrumentality.

CHAPTER FOUR

THE PEOPLE OF GOD
(2.1-10)

THE mention of 'love of the brethren' and the reciprocal 'one another' in 1.22 and the use of terms that had previously been applied to the people of Israel have indicated that it is not isolated individuals but a community that is being addressed. 1 Peter 1 has presupposed the existence of a community, but so far nothing has been said about it directly. With 2.1-10 its shape becomes clear. This section is concerned with the Church—though the actual word 'church' is not used in the letter at all.

This is rather an involved passage. So we had better first try to get an idea of its general structure. Verses 1-3 form the transition from chapter 1, gathering up the preceding exhortation and preparing the way for what follows. The backbone of the section consists of verses 4, 5 and 9, which (1) make it clear that to come to Christ involves of necessity incorporation into a community, (2) describe the nature of that community, and (3) describe its functions. Verses 6-8 are a parenthesis in illustration of 'stone' in 4, while 10 is best taken as a further explanation of the phrase 'of him who called you out of darkness into his marvellous light', which itself is substituted for 'of God', in order to indicate the nature of 'the excellencies' (i.e. mighty acts) referred to in 9.

The ground of appeal in the transitional exhortation is expressed twice, first in a general way by the word 'therefore' indicating that it is in view of what has already been said in the previous chapter that they must lay aside all wickedness, etc., and secondly by verse 3, which rounds off this part of the section. Peter begins: PUTTING AWAY THEREFORE ALL WICKEDNESS ('wickedness' is a comprehensive word for all the evil of the pagan world), AND ALL GUILE (i.e. all that is not straightforward, all devious means

43

and crooked ways in dealing with other people), AND HYPOCRISIES. . . . 'Hypocrisy' means acting a part. We are hypocrites, when what we really are and our real motives belie our outward seeming; and the most alarming thing about it is that we can so very easily deceive ourselves as well as others. We do not have to be engaged in what is called 'church-work' very long, to discover what a perennial source of trouble the next item on the list is—AND ENVIES. It was already troubling the Twelve, while Jesus was still with them, as Mark 10.41 shows. And we should scarcely be surprised if the difference between those two admirable ladies, Euodia and Syntyche, had something to do with it (Phil. 4.2). The list is brought to an end with AND ALL EVIL SPEAKINGS. It is interesting that the word 'all' is repeated here, though omitted before the last two items. Maybe it is simply for the sake of the rhythm of the sentence. Or was it perhaps because the writer knew how prone we all are to justify to ourselves our own little bit of evil speaking? We all deprecate unkind gossip— especially when it is a matter of other people gossiping about us—but somehow the bit of gossip we want to indulge in is always an exception, and we manage to convince ourselves that it is really for the general good. The word 'all' seems to be put in, to head us off from such rationalizations. 'Evil speakings' includes all disparaging gossip about others.

But it is not enough to renounce what is evil; there must be positive growth in what is good, and that requires true nourishment. So AS NEWBORN BABES, LONG FOR THE SPIRITUAL MILK WHICH IS WITHOUT GUILE, THAT YE MAY GROW THEREBY UNTO SALVATION; . . . It is possible that 'as newborn babes' has no reference to the metaphor of 1.3, 23, and is simply put in for the sake of vividness to complete the milk metaphor that follows, but perhaps, in view of the close proximity of 1.23, it is more likely that there is a connection of thought and that they are addressed as yet babes in the faith (another hint that this part of the letter was originally a sermon to the newly baptized?). At any rate, no half-hearted desire for nourishment will do. They must 'long for' it. The word translated 'long for' is a strong one; it is used in the LXX in Ps. 42.1, 119.174.

The nourishment itself is here called 'spiritual milk'; but the word *logikos*, which the R.V. renders by 'spiritual' is something of a riddle. It only occurs twice in the New Testament, here and in Rom. 12.1, and not at all in the LXX. There is some evidence for the meaning 'spiritual' outside the Bible, and it was a favourite word with the Stoics in the sense of 'belonging to the Logos'. In Rom. 12.1 it presumably means 'spiritual' as opposed to 'material';[1] but in 1 Peter 2.2 there is much to be said for going back to the A.V. translation—'of the word'; for we have just been hearing about the Word of God in 1.23-25, and it seems natural to connect *logikon* in 2.2 with *logou* in 1.23. This has the further advantage of giving a definite meaning, whereas 'the spiritual milk' is decidedly vague. So we venture to prefer the A.V. rendering here, and understand a reference to God's Word as the true milk,[2] on which we are to be fed. It is to be pure and unadulterated, free from the admixture of any alien substance (that is the meaning of the word rendered 'which is without guile'). If we are fed on that pure food, we shall thrive and grow up into maturity and finally inherit salvation. It is both a guarantee and at the same time a warning against all substitutes!

Verse 3 rounds off this transitional exhortation: IF YE HAVE TASTED THAT THE LORD IS GRACIOUS. It can have a double significance: 'seeing that you have tasted . . . therefore you must . . .' and also 'if it is really true that you have tasted . . . then you will . . .' (in other words, 'here is the way to prove that you really have tasted . . .'). It is a quotation from Ps. 34.8 (slightly modified). Because they have experienced the goodness of the Lord, and to show that they really have experienced it, they must put away all wickedness, etc.

This transitional exhortation concluded, we now pass on to the main body of the section. Its theme is the Church, the people of God, the new Israel. The first thing that is indicated (by the section as a whole as much as by particular words) is that to come to Christ involves of necessity

[1] Unless it means 'intelligent'—i.e. such as a true understanding of what God has done for us in Christ demands.

[2] For the metaphorical use of 'milk' cf. Isa. 55.1, 1 Cor. 3.2, etc.

incorporation into a community. UNTO WHOM COMING, A LIVING STONE, REJECTED INDEED OF MEN, BUT WITH GOD ELECT, PRECIOUS, YE ALSO AS LIVING STONES, ARE BUILT UP A SPIRITUAL HOUSE. . . . The living Stone implies the living stones, the Foundation implies the edifice that is built upon it, the Elect One implies the elect ones (1.1) not in isolation but as an elect race (2.9). The man, who wants to follow Christ, is willy-nilly ' let in for ' Christ's Church. To accept the Redeemer means also accepting the people whom He has redeemed. The free-lance Christian, who would be a Christian but is too superior to belong to the visible Church on earth in one of its forms, is simply a contradiction in terms. Everywhere the Bible presupposes a people of God, a living organism. That is every bit as true of the New Testament as of the Old. The Scriptures know nothing of an individual piety that is out of touch with the living body of God's people. ' Outside the Church there is no salvation ' is binding on us—though, of course, God is not bound by it.

In the second place, the nature of this community is described, and the words, with which the necessity of the Church have been indicated, must be considered again for the light they throw upon its nature. The first and most important thing about the nature of the Church is indicated by the word ' whom ' in verse 4. ' Whom ' refers to Christ, and the main thing about the Church is that it is Christ's. Apart from Him there is no Church. It is made up of those who come to Christ, and allow themselves to be incorporated into His body. Or in different terms, it is Christ as the foundation and Christ present with His people as their living Lord that makes them the people of God. He is the ' living stone ', upon which the Church is built. Jesus had applied to Himself (Mark 12.10f.) the words of Ps. 118.22: ' The stone which the builders rejected is become the head of the corner '; and it is His use of the words of the Psalm that lies behind the use of ' stone ' here. Cf. Acts 4.11, Eph. 2.20. This stone has been rejected by men, by the high priests and the elders and by the people of Israel after the flesh. He is still rejected by many to-day, who set aside as useless the true Foundation-stone, and try to build their Babel towers upon other foundations. But the stone, which the foolish builders set aside, is 'with God elect, precious'. The words 'elect, precious' come from the LXX version of Isa. 28.16 (the Hebrew, followed by the R.V., is a little different). 'Elect' or 'chosen' (one word in Hebrew and Greek) was applied in the Old Testament to the people of Israel; it was applied also to the Suffering Servant, and to the faithful remnant, and to David frequently, and also to Solomon, Zerubbabel, etc. In Apocalyptic it was applied to the Messiah. Luke 9.35 ('This is my Son, my chosen') and 23.35, where the rulers scoff at Jesus' Messianic claims ('He saved others; let him save himself, if this is the Christ of God, his chosen'), are significant for the associations of the word (cf. Deut. 17.15, Ps. 89.3, 19f., Isa. 42.1). The other word, translated 'precious', has rather the meaning, 'honourable', 'held in esteem'. Though dishonoured by men, He is honoured by God.

Those who come to Christ, the living Stone, themselves become living stones, that are built together upon Him into a spiritual temple.[1] Behind this picture of the Church as a temple, which occurs also in Eph. 2.19-22, 1 Cor. 3.16f., 6.19, 2 Cor. 6.16, there lies the saying of Jesus, 'Destroy this temple, and in three days I will raise it up' (John 2.19-22, cf. Mark 14.58, 15.29). The temple on Mount Zion that was made with hands is replaced by the true temple made without hands, the body of Christ. The true temple of God is the risen, exalted, Christ Himself together with those who as His members share in His risen life. This new temple is indeed 'spiritual', both as contrasted with the temple that was made with hands, and as being the dwelling-place of the Holy Spirit.[2]

We shall leave the latter part of verse 5—TO BE A HOLY PRIESTHOOD, TO OFFER UP SPIRITUAL SACRIFICES, ACCEPTABLE TO GOD THROUGH JESUS CHRIST—for the moment, and deal with it later along with verse 9b. Verses 6-8 are really notes on the word 'stone' in verse 4 and contain quotations from the Old Testament (LXX) to illustrate its meaning. They begin with a quotation from Isa. 28.16: BECAUSE IT IS CONTAINED IN SCRIPTURE (for all New Testament writers

[1] The word rendered 'house' here in R.V. quite often has the specific meaning 'temple', as e.g. in John 2.17.

[2] Cf. John 4.21-24, Rev. 21.22.

a fundamental consideration), BEHOLD, I LAY IN ZION A CHIEF CORNER STONE, ELECT, PRECIOUS: AND HE THAT BELIEVETH ON HIM SHALL NOT BE PUT TO SHAME. Then in exposition of this it is pointed out that the word 'precious' ('honourable') describes what the stone is for believers on Christ; FOR YOU THEREFORE WHICH BELIEVE IS THE PRECIOUSNESS (honour): BUT FOR SUCH AS DISBELIEVE there is something different in store, which is indicated by two other quotations, the first being Ps. 118.22 and the second from Isa. 8.14: THE STONE WHICH THE BUILDERS REJECTED, THE SAME WAS MADE THE HEAD OF THE CORNER; AND, A STONE OF STUMBLING, AND A ROCK OF OFFENCE. The second of these quotations is then further explained by the words: FOR THEY STUMBLE AT THE WORD, BEING DISOBEDIENT: WHEREUNTO ALSO THEY WERE APPOINTED.[1] Christ is both the Foundation-stone, upon which the Church is built, and at the same time He is the One, by their attitude to whom men are judged.

After this digression in illustration of the 'stone', St. Peter goes on with his description of the nature of the Church. BUT (in contrast with those who disbelieve) YE ARE AN ELECT RACE, A ROYAL PRIESTHOOD, A HOLY NATION, A PEOPLE FOR GOD'S OWN POSSESSION. All four phrases come from the Old Testament. They are a weaving together of Exod. 19.5f. and Isa. 43.20f. The titles of Israel are taken over by the Christian Church; for the Church is the new Israel, the true heir and successor of the old. It is a new people indeed, for the decisive event has at last happened, the Messiah has come; but in an equally significant sense there is but one people of God from the days of Abraham, a people with one continuous life, one history, for the saints of the Old Testament also lived by faith in the Christ to come, in expectation of Him and in the strength of God's promises.

---

[1] These last words reflect the same general idea as is expressed much more fully in Rom. 9. We have not space here to enter into the difficult problem of divine predestination; but any reader who is worried by it would find light and help from Barth's suggestive criticism of Calvin's doctrine. The most convenient place for the English reader to find this is Karl Barth's *The Knowledge of God and the Service of God*, 68-79.

As Israel was God's 'elect (or chosen) race', so is the Church, heir alike of the privileges and the obligations of God's chosen people. Like Israel too it is 'a royal priesthood', i.e. a priesthood belonging to the King, to Christ. But the Church did not use the word *hiereus* (the word for a priest in the LXX) to denote its ministers, but *presbyteros* ('elder'). There was to be no priestly caste to fulfil the Church's priestly functions; the whole Church, not a part of it, was to be a priesthood. The priestly service of the Church was something in which every member was to share. That is the scriptural meaning of the phrase 'the priesthood of all believers', which has unfortunately often been misinterpreted to mean that the Church has no priestly character at all! 'A holy nation' is another appropriated title. We have already seen something of what 'holy' means (Chapter III). It does not mean that the Church is made up of people who are paragons of moral perfection —that would be a futile illusion—but that it is *God's* Church, not a mere human organization, that it is called into being by, and lives by, His pardoning grace, and is dedicated to His service in the world. Lastly, it is 'a people for God's own possession', God's special people, the very meaning of whose existence lies in its being possessed by God. The Greek word translated 'people' here is *laos,* which in the LXX is a technical term for Israel as distinguished from all other peoples. The New Testament writers take it over, once more asserting the continuity of the Church with Israel.

We must now go back to verse 5 (latter part) and see what St. Peter has to say about the function of the Church, which was our third main heading for this section. Here two things are said: first, the Church has a priestly function (verse 5), second, it has a prophetic or evangelistic function (verse 9).

First, then, the priestly: 'to be a holy priesthood (or 'for a holy priestly service'), to offer up spiritual sacrifices, acceptable to God through Jesus Christ'. The Church's priestly service consists of the offering up to God of sacrifices. The answer to the question, 'What are these sacrifices?' is provided by Rom. 12.1. The sacrifice is not to be an animal victim, but our own selves, the whole life of

D

the Church both corporately and severally offered up to God, 'ourselves, our souls and bodies, to be a reasonable, holy, and lively sacrifice unto Thee'. This priestly service of the Church includes the whole life of each member but it has its focus-point in the congregation's worship. Sunday by Sunday, in response to the demonstration of God's love in Word and Sacrament we gather up together our whole life, our daily work, the everyday concerns, and offer it up to God in prayer and praise, our sacrifice of thanksgiving. From this central act, the rest of our life gets its meaning. Seen in its light the humdrum tasks in the home, or in office or factory or school, wear a new splendour, and life becomes a whole. Even the monotonous details, which in themselves seem lowly and menial, are taken up into the Church's worship and offered up to God as a part of that thanksgiving, which God's people render to Him for their redemption.

> *'A servant with this clause*
> *Makes drudgery divine;*
> *Who sweeps a room, as for Thy laws,*
> *Makes that and the action fine.'*

George Herbert's words make clear the significance of the Church's priestly service for our everyday life.

These sacrifices, like the 'house' in the same verse, are called 'spiritual', to distinguish them from 'the blood of bulls and goats', from the sacrifices of the Temple on Mount Zion. A further, and tremendously important, point is added: these sacrifices are 'acceptable to God through Jesus Christ'. It is not in themselves that they are acceptable. It is not that the offering of our lives is something so splendid and precious that God cannot help but be pleased with it! On the contrary, our best is feeble and unworthy and stained and spoiled. It is not in themselves that these sacrifices are acceptable to God, but 'through Jesus Christ', when joined to His perfect sacrifice of Himself and offered in His Name. The dignity and splendour of the humblest and most dreary tasks of our everyday life, as of the noblest things we do, lie in this, that they may not only be taken up into the whole offering of the universal

Church, but—something yet more wonderful—actually joined to the one holy and perfect sacrifice that was offered up on Calvary.

The other function of the Church—the prophetic or evangelistic—is set forth in verse 9: THAT YE MAY SHEW FORTH THE EXCELLENCIES (or 'mighty works') OF HIM WHO CALLED YOU OUT OF DARKNESS INTO HIS MARVELLOUS LIGHT. . . . Israel had been called to be the Lord's witnesses to the heathen (Isa. 43.10, 12, 44.8). Now the Church had inherited Israel's missionary vocation. Every member is to be a witness to Christ, and his witnessing, like his priestly service, is a matter of his whole life. We are called to confess Christ by word and deed, at home, at work, in public affairs and social contacts. Again, this activity has its focus-point in the public services of the local congregation, when the Word of God is preached; and each member has a share of responsibility for that corporate witness. The member who is absent from his place, when the congregation bears its public witness, may be likened to the soldier, who is absent without leave, when his unit goes into action. But notice that the content of our evangelism is really to be the mighty works of God in Christ, not mere good advice!

Verse 10—WHICH IN TIME PAST WERE NO PEOPLE, BUT NOW ARE THE PEOPLE OF GOD: WHICH HAD NOT OBTAINED MERCY, BUT NOW HAVE OBTAINED MERCY—recalls Hos. 1.6, 9, 10, 2.1, 23. It is added, in order to indicate something of the meaning of 'out of darkness into his glorious light' and the contrast between the 'now' of the Gospel and the 'time past'. The words of Hos. 2.23, which speak of God's reversal of his disowning of unfaithful Israel, have been fulfilled in Jesus Christ; and not only on Israel, but on gentiles too, has this blessing been bestowed.

CHAPTER FIVE

SOJOURNERS AND PILGRIMS
(2.11-12)

BELOVED is a form of address frequently used by New Testament writers. Probably it was the usual term for addressing the congregation in sermons. It sums up the central motif of the Christian life, indicating at the same time the love of the speaker or writer for his brethren and, behind that and more important, the love of God in Christ for all. Its introduction here suggests that the writer is conscious of moving on to a new division of his letter. These two verses are in fact the introduction to a whole group of sections, which deal with the Christian's obedience in various relationships and together form a main division of the letter. This main division consists of exhortation, and follows from the doctrinal section on the Church. The words, I BESEECH YOU, introduce ethical teaching that is grounded in doctrine, the drawing out of the practical moral implications of the Gospel. Much of it probably represents catechetical material in common use in the early Church, as is indicated by the close parallels in other Epistles.

The readers are appealed to as SOJOURNERS AND PILGRIMS. The two Greek words *paroikos* and *parepidemos* have much the same meaning. The word here translated 'pilgrims' was rendered 'sojourners' in 1.1, and in 1.17 we had the abstract noun formed from the other word. *Parepidemos* emphasizes the transitoriness of the sojourning, while *paroikos* emphasizes the sojourner's legal position as a non-citizen, a resident alien. The two words occur together in Gen. 23.4 (LXX). Abraham says to the children of Heth: 'I am a stranger (*paroikos*) and a sojourner (*parepidemos*) with you'. Abraham had gone out from his native place on a pilgrimage, not knowing whither he went, in obedience to the divine command (Gen.

52

12.1f.). The writer to the Hebrews looks back to Abraham, the father of the faithful: 'By faith Abraham, when he was called, obeyed to go out unto a place which he was to receive for an inheritance; and he went out, not knowing whither he went. By faith he became a sojourner in the land of promise, as in a land not his own, dwelling in tents . . . for he looked for the city which hath foundations, whose builder and maker is God' (Heb. 11.8-10). He goes on in the same chapter, speaking of the patriarchs: 'These all died in faith, not having received the promises, but having seen them and greeted them from afar, and having confessed that they were strangers and pilgrims on the earth' (11.13, cf. Ps. 39.12[1]). That was true of all the saints of Israel. And, say the New Testament writers, it is true equally for the new Israel, for the Church: 'We have not here an abiding city' (Heb. 13.14). So here in 1 Peter the readers are appealed to 'as sojourners and pilgrims'. But there is another side to all this. The saints are strangers and aliens for a reason; and the reason is that they belong elsewhere. So the writer to Hebrews links with 'we have not here an abiding city' the sentence, 'but we seek after the city which is to come' (13.14, cf. 11.14-16). Compare Phil. 3.20—'our citizenship is in heaven'.

This motif of earthly pilgrimage and heavenly citizenship dominates the Christian understanding of life. We are in the world, but not of it; children of light for the time being living as strangers in the darkness. So conscious of this were the early Christians, that the word *paroikia* (translated 'sojourning' in 1.17) came to be a regular term for a Christian congregation (hence our word 'parish'), and they likened the Church's life on earth to Israel's captivity in Babylonia. But there is always a tendency for the Church to settle down and make itself at home in 'Babylon', becoming more and more acclimatized and accommodating itself to the ways of thinking that are characteristic of Babylon, being conformed to the fashion of this world, just as sometimes a British settler in some far corner of the earth may forget the traditions and standards of his home-country and 'go native'. When Christians 'go native' in

---

[1] One of the most important manuscripts of the LXX has 'in the earth' here instead of 'with thee'.

this world, it means that they have forgotten the home-country and the heavenly citizenship.

But, if we are conscious of our citizenship and therefore know ourselves to be strangers here, then we shall understand our inescapable obligation TO ABSTAIN FROM FLESHLY LUSTS. 'Flesh' is here used in its Pauline sense. It means, not a lower element of human nature to be identified with the body, as though that were specially evil, but rather the whole of human nature in its fallen state, organized as it is in alienation from God. It denotes the whole man in his fallenness, not a part of him. So, when Paul lists the 'works of the flesh' in Gal. 5.19ff., many of them have no particular connection with the body, but are rather what we might call spiritual sins, as enmities, jealousies, factions, etc. So here too 'fleshly lusts' includes a much wider range of desires than is usually meant to-day by the lusts of the flesh. The tremendous stress on subordination in the following sections would suggest that the writer has in mind especially man's self-assertiveness, which is so destructive of community and needs to be sternly curbed by the sense of responsibility to, and for, other people.

The fleshly lusts are forces, WHICH WAR AGAINST THE SOUL. 'Soul' (Greek—*psyche*) is sometimes used in the New Testament to denote the natural life, and the adjective *psychikos* always denotes 'natural' as opposed to *pneumatikos* (spiritual, i.e. indwelt by the Holy Spirit); but at other times 'soul' has the sense of 'person' (e.g. Rom. 13.1). Quite often *psyche* is used as equivalent to a reflexive pronoun (e.g. Mark 8.35ff.). Here and in the other places in 1 Peter where it occurs (1.9, 22, 2.25, 4.19) it has a similar meaning. It denotes a man's self, his individuality. While 'flesh' describes him in his alienation from God, 'soul' describes him simply as a self or person. It is this 'soul' that is the object of redemption according to 1.9, 2.25. In the picture of the warfare of the Christian life in Gal. 5.16ff. the two protagonists are the Holy Spirit and the flesh, but there is a third party mentioned—the individual Galatian Christian, who is not just identical with his flesh, but is distinguished from it in St. Paul's use of the second person plural ('walk', 'ye shall not fulfil', 'that ye may not do the things that ye would', 'if ye are led . . . ye are not under the law'). The 'soul' here in 1 Peter is equivalent to the 'ye' in the Galatians passage.

In each Christian's life a war is being waged, or rather it is one scene of operations in the great war between God and evil. The town of Mansoul (the Christian's self) has long been in enemy hands, occupied territory. But outside in the great war the enemy has suffered a decisive defeat—the decisive defeat—and the possession of Mansoul is being disputed. Christ, the victor of the great decisive battle, has sent the Holy Spirit to establish a bridgehead in occupied territory and gain a footing in Mansoul. The bridgehead has been established, and the town has been called to rise up and attack the occupying troops (the fleshly lusts). And now a deadly combat is going on in Mansoul between the occupation troops on the one side and on the other, the Holy Spirit, the liberator, assisted by the citizens.

The writer goes on to adapt the words of Jesus in Matt. 5.16 to the situation of his readers, giving a particular reference to the general thought. HAVING YOUR BEHAVIOUR SEEMLY AMONG THE GENTILES; THAT, WHEREIN THEY SPEAK AGAINST YOU AS EVIL-DOERS, THEY MAY BY YOUR GOOD WORKS, WHICH THEY BEHOLD, GLORIFY GOD IN THE DAY OF VISITATION. They are to reply to the malicious slanders of the pagans by living lives of such exemplary goodness that even their slanderers will finally be won over. False accusation is always a favourite weapon of the Church's persecutors, and there is a long story of the slanders made against Christians, from charges of cannibalism and incest in the earliest days down to those of misusing the pulpit for political purposes, being unpatriotic, committing currency offences and espionage. But there are also the less spectacular charges that are made by those who are hostile, but can hardly be called persecutors, charges of hypocrisy, of being kill-joys, and narrow-minded. Many are the prejudices and misunderstandings, which help to keep men away from the Church. They are to be overcome by the convincing argument of lives that are good and gracious. Too often our lives tell in the opposite direction—members of the same congregation who refuse to speak to each other, competitive spirit between the denominations, doubtful business dealings by Church members, and so on.

The exact significance of ' in the day of visitation ' is not certain. It is unlikely that it refers to the day when the Christians will be brought to trial in court; for in the Bible the subject of 'visit' is generally God Himself. But it might refer to God's visiting the Christians concerned or their slanderers. In the first case it would presumably mean visiting them in mercy and delivering them from their persecutors; in the second, it might mean visiting them in judgment and punishing them, or else in mercy opening their eyes to the truth. Or it may simply refer in a general way to the final Day of Judgment.

CHAPTER SIX

CHRISTIAN CITIZEN

(2.13-17)

ACCORDING to the R.V. the new section begins: BE SUB-
JECT TO EVERY ORDINANCE OF MAN FOR THE LORD'S
SAKE. But it is unlikely that 'ordinance of man' is
the correct translation of the two Greek words it represents.
The word rendered 'ordinance' (*ktisis*) is derived from the
verb *ktizo*, and elsewhere in the New Testament this verb
and its derivatives are used only of God's creating. In view
of this and the evidence of the LXX it seems unlikely that
ktisis here can mean an ordinance appointed by man. Hort
tried to get over the difficulty by rendering the words
'divine institution among men', but that involves a somewhat forced interpretation of the adjective *anthropinos*
('human'), and, moreover, no example of *ktisis* meaning
'ordinance' or 'order' with reference to the state (whether
regarded as a divine or a human ordinance) has yet been
adduced either from classical or biblical Greek. Its natural
biblical meaning is 'creation' or 'creature'. The difficulties disappear as soon as we realize that this part of
verse 13 has a more general reference and is to be taken as a
heading to the whole group of sections in which the idea of
subordination plays an important part. We can then render
ktisis by 'creature', its proper meaning, and the adjective
anthropinos will then indicate that of creatures it is human
beings that are intended. So we get the sentence, 'Be
subject to every man for the Lord's sake', as a general
heading to the main division (2.13-3.12) concerned with
the Christian's duty in the various relationships of this
life.[1]

Fallen man's natural reaction to his fellows is to assert
himself and attempt to exploit others for his own self-

[1] Cf. W. Foerster in Kittel's *Theol. Woerterbuch zum N.T.*, III,
1034.

aggrandisement.   An attitude and spirit diametrically
opposed to this must be characteristic of those who are
sojourners and pilgrims in this world and whose citizenship
is in heaven. This Christian attitude is denoted by the key-
word 'be subject', which is used in this verse and again in
2.18, 3.1 (cf. the similar idea in 3.7, 8f.). It signifies a
voluntary subordination of oneself to others, putting the
interests and welfare of others above one's own, preferring
to give rather than to receive, to serve rather than to be
served; 'subjecting yourselves one to another in the fear
of Christ' (Eph. 5.21), 'in honour preferring one another'
(Rom. 12.10), 'in lowliness of mind each counting other·
better than himself; not looking each of you to his own
things, but each of you also to the things of others' (Phil.
2.3f.). It means a giving oneself to, and for, others. It
is, in fact, to follow in the steps of Him, who disdained
not to be His brother's keeper, but for the sake of His
brethren went to the cross. From what has been said it
should be clear that this being subject does not mean yield-
ing an unquestioning obedience to others: that is something
quite different.

Of course, it is possible for us to be self-seeking even in
our unselfishness! There is such a thing as an unselfishness that is only a refined form of self-assertion, an unselfishness that does not spring from love and therefore is
but sounding brass and a clanging cymbal. The words
'for the Lord's sake' forbid all such hypocrisy. Our unselfishness is to be the real thing, springing from our sense
of our own infinite indebtedness to our Lord—really for
His sake, and so really self-forgetting. 'For the Lord's
sake' indicates the one thing that is able to set us free for
this subordination of ourselves to others. It is gratitude to
Him, that is to enable us to accept gladly and unreservedly
the neighbour to whom He has bound us in the varied
relationships of His appointing.

We pass now from the general to the particular. The
Christian, though his citizenship is in heaven, is also a
citizen of a particular earthly State. How then is this Christian attitude of subordination of oneself to others to be
expressed in this relationship? It will mean readily and
ungrudgingly and for the Lord's sake shouldering his re-

sponsibilities and recognizing in the lawful claims of the State part of his obligation to his neighbour. The Christian is to be subject, then, WHETHER IT BE TO THE KING (i.e. the Roman Emperor), AS SUPREME; OR UNTO GOVERNORS (i.e. of provinces), AS SENT BY HIM. . . . The original reference was to Nero—so the citizen's obligation is not dependent on the personal goodness of the ruler, but on the office or function. St. Peter then sums up the purpose of the State in God's intention: it is FOR VENGEANCE ON EVIL-DOERS AND FOR PRAISE TO THEM THAT DO WELL. It is to restrain the disruptive and chaotic tendencies of men's self-assertion, to encourage well-doing and discourage evil-doing by providing human selfishness with selfish reasons (i.e. reasons which it can understand) for doing right (rewards, 'praise') and for not doing wrong (fear of punishment, 'vengeance'). The motives, to which the State appeals, are not the highest, for the State (even a Christian State) is not the Church, but includes those who deliberately reject the Gospel. It is a provision of God's mercy for fallen man, for the curbing of the worst excesses of man's sinfulness and the maintenance of a degree of order in a world disrupted by man's disobedience. It is subsidiary to the divine reconciliation of men through Christ, which it is meant to serve by maintaining those outward conditions under which the Gospel can be preached unhindered. So in 1 Tim. 2.1-7 the State is connected, not with creation, but with redemption. Therefore the Christian must fulfil his obligations to the State, knowing its true purpose, not just from those selfish motives (of 'praise' and 'vengeance'), which make their appeal to unbelievers, but 'for conscience sake' (Rom. 13.5), 'for the Lord's sake', as part of his service of Jesus Christ. But he must always bear in mind the very necessary proviso of Acts 4.19, 5.29. The government may from time to time order what God forbids. Then the Christian will show his real loyalty to the government by disobeying its unlawful commands. Or—what is worse—a government may, not just occasionally, but systematically and deliberately turn its back on justice and encourage injustice, it may attempt to usurp God's place; it may cease to be the restraining power of 2 Thess. 2.6 and become the beast out of the abyss of Rev. 13. But, provided that the State to which he belongs is fulfilling its true function as a State (whether it is a Christian or a secular State), the Christian is under an obligation of loyalty to it.

At this point we must notice a significant difference between the situation envisaged by the New Testament writers and our own. They were thinking in terms of an authoritarian State, which was the only form of State they had to deal with, and therefore regard the citizen solely as a subject, whose duty to the State was mainly passive, a matter of obedience and paying taxes. We live under a different form of State—a democracy, which needs from its citizens not merely respect for authority and submission to taxation, but an active and responsible co-operation. The citizen is not merely a subject; he actually shares in the responsibility of government. We have no reason to think that a democracy is any less acceptable to God as a form of human State than an authoritarian State. On the contrary, there are reasons for thinking that democracy agrees better with the Christian understanding of man. It follows then that we must interpret the New Testament requirement of subjection to include (in our situation) responsible political activity, the responsible choice of representatives in parliamentary and municipal elections, a serious effort to understand political issues, and to help to form an intelligent public opinion. To these we must probably add readiness under certain circumstances to join in military action; for it would seem that a fundamental refusal here amounts to a fundamental refusal of the State as such. To fail in this wider application of ' subjection ' would for us be disobedience to the New Testament teaching.[1]

St. Peter continues: FOR SO IS THE WILL OF GOD, THAT BY WELL-DOING YE SHOULD PUT TO SILENCE THE IGNORANCE OF FOOLISH MEN. By being good citizens those Christians in Asia Minor were to do what in them lay to shut the mouths of their slanderers. That was an additional reason.

But there must have been many in the early Church, who, having learned the word freedom as a catchword of their

[1] For what the New Testament has to say about the State see further Mark 12.13-17, John 18.28-19.16, Rom. 13.1-7, 1 Tim. 2.1-7, Rev. 13. See also K. Barth, *Church and State*, S.C.M. Press; W. A. Visser 't Hooft, *The Kingship of Christ*, S.C.M. Press.

new faith, would not have relished Peter's emphasis on subjection. To such people the Apostle says: Yes, you are indeed free. Let your service be rendered freely, not degraded by a sense of compulsion. You are free, but do not use your new freedom as an excuse for wickedness. Free—yes, but you are God's slaves! It is His bond-service that is your perfect freedom. AS FREE, AND yet NOT USING YOUR FREEDOM FOR A CLOKE OF WICKEDNESS, BUT AS BOND-SERVANTS OF GOD.

The section is summed up in four brief commands: HONOUR ALL MEN. LOVE THE BROTHERHOOD. FEAR GOD. HONOUR THE KING. The first is equivalent to what we saw to be the true meaning of the first part of verse 13. We have a duty towards all men, to honour them as our neighbours, as men for whom Christ died, and never to exploit them as mere means to some end of our own, but to treat them always as ends in themselves, as persons. Within the wider area there is an inner circle, the Christian brotherhood, in which the uniting bond is closer, and in which Christ's peace is to reign. The last two commands are taken from Prov. 24.21—but with a difference. In Proverbs we have 'My son, fear thou the Lord and the king'; but Peter will not use the same verb to denote what is owed to the Emperor and what is owed to God; for what we owe to God is unique. The king is to be honoured, but God is to be feared. In 1 Peter the object of 'fear' is always God, except where the fear spoken of is one that is to be laid aside.

CHAPTER SEVEN

CHRISTIAN SLAVE

(2.18-25)

THIS section is addressed to SERVANTS, i.e. slaves. The word used is not the general word for a slave, but one that denotes a household slave as opposed to a slave employed in a labour-gang in industry or large-scale agriculture.

The institution of slavery was universal in the ancient world and was the foundation of ancient society and economy. In the earlier stages of Greek and Latin civilization the number of slaves had been quite small, but the system had a natural tendency to grow. The great wars of Rome brought in huge numbers of prisoners of war to be sold on the slave-market. After a big victory the market might be flooded. But the increasing supply stimulated an increasing demand, which in times of peace far exceeded the 'legitimate' supply. So systematic kidnapping was carried on. In New Testament times in Rome and other great cities the slaves would be well over half the population. It should be remembered that many of them were well-educated; the doctors, school-masters, secretaries, clerks would normally be slaves. Those employed in the labour-gangs lived under appalling conditions and were literally worked to death with the utmost heartlessness. But the lot of domestic slaves was usually very much better, and the abominable cruelties we sometimes hear of were exceptional. Quite often there was real affection between master and slave. But the slave had no rights. He was a mere chattel. He could be tortured or put to death by his master for any offence or for no offence. The normal method of execution for a slave was crucifixion. In court his evidence was only valid if given under torture. His marriage had no legal force; his children belonged to his master. When old or sick, and so no longer useful, he might be left to die of exposure. Slavery was taken for granted as something natural—Aristotle argued that some men were by nature slaves, others free—and it was taken for granted that slaves had no rights at all, though some moralists did urge kindness and considerateness towards them. Here and there a voice was raised to question the justice of the institution, as, for example, that of the tragedian Euripides. It was after the time of 1 Peter that Stoic influence led the Emperors to introduce legislation to give some rights to slaves. In Israel the conditions of slaves had always been better, and they had some important rights, e.g. if circumcised, they partook of the Passover with their masters. Moreover, to kill a slave was murder. And there was not the same contempt for manual work, as something beneath the dignity of free men.

St. Peter addresses himself to the Christian slaves, but, unlike St. Paul, he does not go on to a complementary exhortation directed to Christian masters, perhaps because there were not many of them in the churches, to which his letter was to go, or perhaps because he did not feel that their position presented so urgent a personal problem, or perhaps because he was concentrating attention more particularly on the humbler side of each relationship. His counsel to the Christian slaves is: BE IN SUBJECTION TO YOUR MASTERS. He does not discuss the institution of slavery (nor does any New Testament writer), but simply addresses himself to the immediate personal problems of the slave who is a Christian, and bids him do the only thing practicable—in a Christian spirit.

Some people are quite naturally puzzled by the failure of the New Testament writers to denounce an institution to our minds so contradictory to the Gospel. But it must be remembered that they were for the most part addressing slaves, and to denounce the system to them would have been either useless or else much worse; for the slaves had no peaceful constitutional way of protesting and if they attempted to free themselves, that could only mean a bitter and futile servile war. Such servile wars there had been, as for instance that generally called the Second Servile War, in which a force of 40,000 slaves had been defeated by

Lucullus; but the result was always the same, the slaves were defeated, and then the roads far and wide were lined with crosses bearing the rotting bodies of the slaves, and afterwards masters were all the more oppressive and vindictive, fearing a fresh outbreak. To incite Christian slaves—or pagan slaves, for that matter—to revolt would have been to condemn them to certain death, and to increase the hardships and sufferings of those who did not revolt.

The tiny and outwardly insignificant Church of the first century could not hope to effect the immediate abolition of slavery. So, in the meantime, instead of staging a suicidal attempt, it set about doing what was practicable and bringing to the slave the liberty of Christ and a dignity that drew the sting from his humiliations. At least within the Christian community the ugly thing was transformed, and thereby the very institution of slavery was surely, if slowly, undermined. If Onesimus was not freed after his return to Colossae, we can at least be certain that his slavery was something very different from what it once had been. In the Church's fellowship the distinction between freeman and slave was no longer important; for it was realized that in Christ there can be neither bond nor free. So slave and freeman were brothers beloved, exchanged with each other the kiss of peace, drank from the same chalice, suffered the same martyrdom, looked forward to the same heavenly inheritance. There was nothing surprising to Christians, when an ex-slave Callistus became bishop of Rome, or the lady Perpetua and the slave-girl Felicitas faced death together in the arena hand in hand; for the miracle had already happened. Even where the master was heathen, the slave's position was altogether transformed, if he were a Christian himself; for he was already free in Christ, and the old humiliations and sufferings were now no longer sordid, but were part of his following in the steps of Christ, who, though He was God, had taken the form of a slave, suffered the slave's punishment of scourging, and died a slave's death upon the cross. So inwardly he was free, and was able to make out of the cruel wrong he had to suffer, a positive good.

But it would be quite disingenuous to argue from Peter's

exhortation here (or from the general attitude of the New Testament to the institution of slavery) that therefore to-day strikes are necessarily un-Christian or that the under-dog should never resist exploitation or that the indirect and gradual method, which was the only practicable one for a tiny persecuted minority, must be also right for the Church in a Christian or at least nominally Christian country. It would indeed be handling the Word of God deceitfully to seek to justify our own failures to speak boldly against modern evils by 'slaves, be in subjection to your masters'. But to say this is not to say that this passage has no message for us to-day. We shall see very soon that it has.

The slaves are to be subject to their masters WITH ALL FEAR—i.e. fear of God, not of their masters (cf. 'for conscience toward God' in the next verse). And that, NOT ONLY TO THE GOOD AND GENTLE, BUT ALSO TO THE FROWARD. They are to offer up to God their daily submission to their masters, and therefore that submission is to be independent of their masters' worthiness or unworthiness. We may apply this to ourselves. Honest and diligent work and a courteous attitude are good in themselves; we are not to be more or less honest and diligent in our work or courteous in our attitude according to whether our employer is more or less worthy; but rather to work properly and be courteous, because we want to please God. St. Peter continues: FOR THIS IS ACCEPTABLE, IF FOR CONSCIENCE TOWARD GOD A MAN ENDURETH GRIEFS, SUFFERING WRONGFULLY. FOR WHAT GLORY IS IT, IF, WHEN YE SIN, AND ARE BUFFETED FOR IT, YE SHALL TAKE IT PATIENTLY? BUT IF, WHEN YE DO WELL, AND SUFFER FOR IT, YE SHALL TAKE IT PATIENTLY, THIS IS ACCEPT-ABLE WITH GOD. The words of Jesus recorded in Matt. 5.46-48 and Luke 6.32-35 (it is worthwhile looking at both passages and comparing them carefully) almost certainly are behind St. Peter's words here. There is nothing extra-ordinary (in the Matthew version 'more than others'— Greek *perisson*; in the Luke version the same word is used as here, though the R.V. renders differently—'thank' in Luke 6.32ff., 'acceptable' here) in bearing patiently suffer-ings one has deserved. But, when one is innocent, to bear undeserved sufferings patiently—this is 'extraordinary'.

E

And the 'extraordinary' is a characteristic of the Christian,[1] who is bidden to go the extra mile and to turn the other cheek and to love his enemy. The secret of this is revealed in the following verses.

FOR HEREUNTO WERE YE CALLED: (this meekness and patience in bearing undeserved sufferings are your high calling in Christ) BECAUSE CHRIST ALSO SUFFERED FOR YOU, . . . Here is the supreme motive—the consciousness of an infinite indebtedness to Christ, the sense of gratitude to Him for what He has done 'for you'. 'For you', on your behalf, implies that Christ's sufferings and death were much more than an example (though that they certainly were, as St. Peter's next words will emphasize). His sufferings were vicarious. (It is probable that Isa. 53.4 was in the writer's mind; for there the LXX text has 'and suffers for us', where the R.V. renders the Hebrew text 'and carried our sorrows'.) St. Peter's words imply that the cross provides not only the motive or reason for this meekness that he is urging, but also the moral strength. It provides also the pattern to be copied—LEAVING YOU AN EXAMPLE, THAT YE SHOULD FOLLOW HIS STEPS. The disciple is to follow in the footprints of his Lord. The Christian life is an 'imitation of Christ'.

This bringing of the sordid humiliations and sufferings of Christian slaves into direct association with Christ's cross is the heart of this section. The slave, whom the pagan world regarded as base and ignoble in spirit as well as status, is invited to the imitation of Christ, to the same high calling as the Christian freeman. That meant, of course, his moral and spiritual emancipation. What was sordid in itself—the indignities inflicted by a selfish master—became something dignified and noble, when seen as a following in Christ's footsteps. It is just here that we must look for the main message of this section for ourselves. It tells us that our sufferings too may be transformed from the meaningless and maybe sordid thing that they often are into something of dignity and worth by being associated with Christ's sufferings and that our little crosses may be lit up by the splendour and brightness of His cross. This applies

[1] Cf. D. Bonhoeffer: *The Cost of Discipleship*, S.C.M. Press, 126-133.

to those wrongs and humiliations, that we may sometimes have to bear, if our circumstances have placed a large measure of power over our lives in someone else's hands. There are many such situations in the modern world. Those of prisoners of war and civilians under military occupation are extreme examples; but there is no lack of petty tyrants in most spheres. A single chevron can very easily go to a man's head and even ecclesiastical power has sometimes a tendency to corrupt. But we may also apply the message of this section much more generally; for all sufferings, small or great, may become meaningful and dignified when accepted in the light of Christ's cross.

The language with which the divine Sufferer is described in verses 22 to 24 derives partly from Isa. 53 and partly from the memory of an eye-witness of the Passion. The account of Christ's sufferings is consciously and deliberately set in the context of the Old Testament foreshadowing. The divine Sufferer was sinless, the one altogether innocent Sufferer—WHO DID NO SIN, NEITHER WAS GUILE FOUND IN HIS MOUTH (cf. Isa. 53.9). In verse 23 there is no actual quotation of the Old Testament, though Isa. 53.7 may well have been in the writer's mind, and perhaps also Ps. 69.9; the language suggests rather the eye-witness' memory of what had actually happened (perhaps also the reference to 'buffeting' in 20 may be reminiscent of the scene described in Mark 14.65). WHO, WHEN HE WAS REVILED, REVILED NOT AGAIN—we may refer to Mark 14.65, 15.17-20, 29-32, which tell of the blindfolding in the court, the mocking by the soldiers, the gibes of the passers-by and of the chief priests, when He was on the cross, and finally of His fellow-crucified, and to Mark 14.61, 15.5, Luke 23.9 for His silence. No bitter threats or prayers for vengeance escaped His dying lips, but instead a prayer to His Father to forgive His enemies (Luke 23.34); He, WHEN HE SUFFERED, THREATENED NOT; BUT in humble trust COMMITTED HIMSELF TO HIM THAT JUDGETH RIGHTEOUSLY (cf. the saying recorded in Luke 23.46, which seems also to lie behind 4.19). The first part of verse 24—WHO HIS OWN SELF BARE OUR SINS IN HIS BODY UPON THE TREE—contains a reminiscence of Isa. 53.12, 'he bare the sin of many' (LXX —'himself bare the sins of many'). The bearing of our sins means suffering the punishment of them in our place (cf. Num. 14.33). On the cross He bore not merely physical pain and sorrow that men could be so blind and wicked, but, what was much more dreadful, that separation from His Father ('My God, my God, why hast thou forsaken me?') that was the due reward of our sins. Next the purpose of the sufferings of Christ is stated—THAT WE, HAVING DIED UNTO SINS, MIGHT LIVE UNTO RIGHTEOUSNESS (cf. Rom. 6.1-11). Christ died in order that we, having been made sharers in His death, might also share His resurrection life. St. Peter may have the sacrament of Baptism in mind, as St. Paul had; that would not imply any Pauline influence, for St. Paul appeals to the fact that his readers have in Baptism died with Christ and been buried with Him as something generally agreed.

Finally the result is described—BY WHOSE STRIPES YE WERE HEALED. FOR YE WERE GOING ASTRAY LIKE SHEEP; BUT ARE NOW RETURNED UNTO THE SHEPHERD AND BISHOP OF YOUR SOULS. Again the language is largely borrowed from Isa. 53.5f. The change back from the first person plural ('that we . . . might live unto righteousness') to the second person is abrupt and emphasizes the special application to slaves. The word rendered 'stripes' means a 'weal', such as often disfigured the bodies of slaves. The Son of God, who had taken the form of a slave, had also suffered the humiliating punishment of a slave. In His scourging and its ugly marks was healing for them, healing both in the sense of comfort in their sufferings and in the deeper sense suggested by the following words. They had in their past life been far from God; but now like lost sheep they have been brought back. The word *episkopos* ('bishop') is probably here used, not in its technical ecclesiastical sense, but in its primary sense of 'one who watches over' as interpreting 'shepherd'. (For the shepherd and sheep metaphor cf. pp. 109f.)

CHAPTER EIGHT

CHRISTIAN WIFE AND CHRISTIAN HUSBAND

(3.1-7)

ST. PETER now turns to the most intimate of all human relationships, addressing himself in 3.1-6 to Christian wives, in 3.7 to Christian husbands. The exhortation to wives is much longer than that to husbands, partly no doubt because women were more numerous than men in these early Christian communities, but chiefly because the position of a Christian wife was usually much more difficult than that of a Christian husband, and the wives were therefore in greater need of pastoral counsel and encouragement. It is assumed that the Christian wives will for the most part have pagan husbands but that the Christian husbands will have Christian wives, it being very much easier, in view of the great authority possessed by the husband in contemporary society, for a husband on becoming a Christian to carry his wife with him than for a wife to carry her husband with her. If a wife did remain pagan, that would not expose her Christian husband to the same harsh treatment as many a Christian woman must have suffered from her pagan husband. We need to bear these historical considerations in mind, as we try to understand this passage. But let no one draw the conclusion that what St. Peter says must therefore be out of date and irrelevant!

It is probable that IN LIKE MANNER is intended simply to indicate that this section is one in a series, and not particularly to press a comparison between the relation of wives to their husbands with that of slaves to their masters.

The words YE WIVES BE IN SUBJECTION TO YOUR OWN HUSBANDS make it plain that this passage is not concerned with the relations between men and women generally, but only with the relation of husband and wife. There is noth-

69

ing here about any general inferiority of women to men. It is important for us to get this quite clear!

The Christian wives are bidden to 'be in subjection' (the theme-word of this whole group of sections—cf. 2.13, 18) to their husbands. But this is to be something very much more than the conventional submissiveness that the ancient world expected of a wife. Outwardly it might seem at first sight to be nothing more; but in reality it is to be something quite different, the expression of that Christian attitude of subordination of self to others, of which we have already heard, not on the level of compulsion or resignation, but something freely given, active, not passive, drawing its strength not from the fear of man but from the Gospel of Christ.

Peter is trying to help the Christian wives of heathen husbands in Asia Minor in the first century A.D. It was no use suggesting that they should explain to their partners that in Christ 'there can be no male and female', though the Church had already grasped that tremendous truth (Gal. 3.28). So he does not embark on any disquisition on the rights of women, but gives them some practical advice. They must conform to the social conventions of the day, in so far as these do not directly conflict with their obedience to Christ. So they are to show the dutifulness that is expected of them. Peter cannot by his letter suddenly alter the legal position of wives in Asia Minor. What he can do is to help these women to see their situation in a new light. If they understand and follow his advice, then their submission to their husbands will be lifted altogether above the level of irksome necessity and perhaps bitter and brutal compulsion to that of real spiritual freedom and willing service of Christ. And at the same time they will be helping to break down the prejudice of pagans against the Church and the Gospel—this was an important consideration with Peter (cf. 2.12, 15). On the other hand, if they were impatient and presumed on their new-found liberty and equality in Christ, then they would cause unnecessary offence and misunderstanding and would make the task of winning a heathen world to Christ harder. So he is anxious that these Christian wives should be above suspicion.

And had not each one of them a very special reason for exemplary dutifulness?—THAT, EVEN IF ANY OBEY NOT THE WORD,[1] THEY MAY WITHOUT THE WORD BE GAINED BY THE BEHAVIOUR OF THEIR WIVES. How could a wife's allegiance to Christ be sincere, if she did not long for her husband's conversion? But how to win him? By word spoken? Yes, of course, she must be ready to speak about Christ. But to persist in talking to someone who does not want to listen only hardens. Then the beauty of a gentle and quiet spirit may—without words being spoken—be more effective than what might only seem a continual nagging, and those whose hearts are proof against preaching may at last be softened by BEHOLDING day by day YOUR CHASTE BEHAVIOUR COUPLED WITH FEAR (i.e. the fear of God, which expresses itself in an unassuming and yet dignified bearing towards others). Neither the motive nor the delicate practical hint is out of date; for Sunday by Sunday there are many in church whose life-partners seldom or never come, and men are still liable to be hardened, if they feel their wives are 'getting at' them.

Verses 3 and 4 deal with the subject of true adornment —WHOSE ADORNING LET IT NOT BE THE OUTWARD ADORNING OF PLAITING THE HAIR, AND OF WEARING JEWELS OF GOLD, OR OF PUTTING ON APPAREL; BUT LET IT BE THE HIDDEN MAN OF THE HEART, IN THE INCORRUPTIBLE APPAREL OF A MEEK AND QUIET SPIRIT, WHICH IS IN THE SIGHT OF GOD OF GREAT PRICE. This does not mean that dowdiness or slovenliness is a Christian virtue. But Peter lays his finger on a weakness characteristic of women—though by no means confined to them. He knows that they are in danger of setting too great store on matters of outward appearance and finery. A Christian woman, while she should not be careless of outward beauty which is God's gift, must not rely upon it, but rather on the inner adornment of a meek and quiet spirit, remembering that the Lord 'seeth not as man seeth; for man looketh on the outward appearance, but the Lord looketh on the heart'. A Christian man or woman needs to keep a sense of proportion in the spending of time and

[1] In 3.1 'the word' is used in two different senses: at its first occurrence it means 'the Word of God', 'the Gospel', at its second occurrence, simply 'speaking'.

money, lest the more important things be sacrificed for the less important.

There follows an appeal to the example of the holy women of old, especially to Sarah, the mother of the faithful (cf. Isa. 51.2); for they adorned themselves with the beauty of a gentle and calm disposition and were dutiful to their own husbands—FOR AFTER THIS MANNER AFORETIME THE HOLY WOMEN ALSO, WHO HOPED IN GOD, ADORNED THEMSELVES, BEING IN SUBJECTION TO THEIR OWN HUS-BANDS: AS SARAH OBEYED ABRAHAM, CALLING HIM LORD (Gen. 18.12). Those, to whom Peter is writing, will show themselves Sarah's true spiritual daughters, gentiles though most of them may be, if they follow her example—WHOSE CHILDREN YE NOW ARE, IF YE DO WELL, AND ARE NOT PUT IN FEAR BY ANY TERROR. There might seem to be a contradiction between the last clause and what was said about fear in verse 2; but there is not, for, while the fear there referred to was the fear of God which carries with it a true reverence for others, what is here meant is the fear of man, of the caprices and spitefulness of a heathen husband. Fearing God, they are to be free from other fears.

And now it is the Christian husbands' turn—YE HUS-BANDS, IN LIKE MANNER, DWELL WITH YOUR WIVES ACCORD-ING TO KNOWLEDGE, GIVING HONOUR UNTO THE WOMAN, AS UNTO THE WEAKER VESSEL. . . . We cannot press 'in like manner', for the word it represents is sometimes only a connecting link between items in a list (cf. on verse 1); but from a comparison of 2.13 and 17 it is clear that 'honour' has much the same force as 'be in subjection to'. The husbands are also called to Christian subordination of self in relation to their wives. We may compare 1 Cor. 7.3f., where the reciprocity of the relationship (when both partners are Christians) is emphasized. 'According to knowledge' may refer to knowledge of God (the point would then be that their treatment of their wives is to be determined by their knowledge of God's character and will) or to practical wisdom and sympathy, understanding of the other person's feelings, etc. The woman is described as 'the weaker vessel',[1] because she is, generally speaking,

[1] The word 'vessel' is not in any way derogatory. It is used of Paul in Acts 9.15. Cf. 2 Tim. 2.21.

physically weaker than the man. In view of the following words, it seems unlikely that any idea of women being intellectually and morally inferior to men is included, though such a general inferiority was usually taken for granted in the ancient world and sometimes very bluntly asserted.

The next phrase is of tremendous significance, not only in connection with marriage but also for the relations of men and women generally. The husbands are bidden to honour their wives—AS BEING ALSO JOINT-HEIRS OF THE GRACE OF LIFE. Where both husband and wife are Christians, they are spiritually equal, having an equal share in the privileges and duties of the Gospel. Here is the true foundation of the emancipation of women. Where it is recognized that husband and wife are spiritual equals, there is an end of domestic tyranny. It means that women are taken seriously as persons, and can no more be thought of, or treated, as mere drudges, mere child-bearing machines, or mere playthings.

A final phrase is added. The husbands must follow the apostolic counsel, because only so will their fellowship with God be advanced—TO THE END THAT YOUR PRAYERS BE NOT HINDERED. Two truths of the utmost importance are contained in those words. The first is that selfishness in the relationship between husband and wife, any form of exploitation of the other person, is a certain way of spoiling the spiritual life. The second is that marriage is only rightly understood and rightly used, when it is clearly recognized that it is not an end in itself but that there is an end more important and more ultimate, which marriage itself is meant to serve, namely, our fellowship with God.

There is one general point that this section makes clear that should be mentioned before we conclude this chapter. Peter is all the time talking about duties rather than rights. Both the wives in 1-6 and the husbands in 7 are told what they are to give, not what they are to claim. He does not say to the husbands: 'Your wives ought to be in subjection to you'—that would be a charter for domestic tyranny! Nor does he say to the wives: 'Your husbands owe you honour, because you are the weaker vessels'. Instead, he bids both think of their duties. It is an unhealthy thing

that so many of us have got into the habit of turning this
upside down, of concentrating all our attention upon our
rights, on the duties of others towards us, on what others
ought to give to us, while thinking as little as possible, if
at all, about our duties and others' rights. It is small wonder when a marriage, in which both partners are obsessed
with their rights, does not prove much of a success!

CHAPTER NINE

CALLED TO INHERIT
A BLESSING

(3.8-12)

VERSES 8-12 form the epilogue to the whole group of sections that began with 2.11. This epilogue sums it all up—FINALLY—by indicating six things which Christians are to be and the reason why, which is then confirmed and illustrated by a quotation from Ps. 34.

First, BE YE ALL LIKEMINDED. The adjective translated 'likeminded' only occurs in the New Testament here, but the idea occurs frequently. Compare Rom .15.5f., Phil. 2.2, 4.2, 1 Cor. 1.10ff., 3.3ff.; and above all the words of Jesus' High-Priestly prayer, 'that they may all be one . . .' (John 17.21ff.).[1] The New Testament never treats this agreeing together in Christ as an unnecessary though highly desirable spiritual luxury, but as something essential to the true being of the Church. Divisions, whether disagreements between individual members or the existence of factions and parties and—how much more!—our present-day denominations, constitute a calling in question of the Gospel itself and a sign that those involved are carnal. The more seriously we take the New Testament, the more urgent and painful becomes our sense of the sinfulness of our divisions, and the more earnest our prayers and strivings after the peace and unity of the Church on earth. That does not mean that the likemindedness we are to strive for is to be a drab uniformity of the sort beloved of bureaucrats. Rather is it to be a unity in which powerful tensions are held together by an overmastering loyalty, and strong antipathies of race and colour, temperament and taste, social position and economic interest, are overcome in common worship

[1] Cf. Acts 4.32, Rom. 12.4f., 16, 1 Cor. 10.17, 12.12ff., 2 Cor. 13.11, Eph. 2.13ff., 4.3ff., Phil. 1.27.

75

and common obedience. Such unity will only come when Christians are humble and bold enough to lay hold on the unity already given in Christ and to take it more seriously than their own self-importance and sin, and to make of those deep differences of doctrine, which originate in our imperfect understanding of the Gospel and which we dare not belittle, not an excuse for letting go of one another or staying apart, but rather an incentive for a more earnest seeking in fellowship together to hear and obey the voice of Christ.

COMPASSIONATE—the word is *sympatheis* (cf. ' sympathy' etc.) and means ' suffering together with others'. It denotes that rejoicing with them that rejoice and weeping with them that weep (Rom. 12.15), which come naturally to those who are conscious of belonging to one body, so that ' whether one member suffereth, all the members suffer with it; or one member is honoured, all the members rejoice with it' (1 Cor. 12.26).

LOVING AS BRETHREN (better ' loving the brethren ')—the fellow-members of the new Israel, like the fellow-members of the old, are brothers. The vertical relationship, God's love to men in Christ, creates a horizontal relationship, the love between those who know themselves to be the objects of the divine love. This brotherly love is the badge of Christians (John 13.35)—and its presence the pledge that we have passed out of death into life (1 John 3.14, cf. 4.20).

TENDERHEARTED—denotes something rare at all times, but perhaps particularly to-day, when we have become so accustomed to hearing and reading of other people's sufferings, that we all are in danger of becoming hardened and brutalized. We got used to hearing on the radio of a thousand-bomber raid as we ate our breakfast. We have got used to the idea of millions of people being refugees. It is not easy now to awaken feelings of pity vivid enough to lead to unselfish action. In such days it is more important than ever that within the Christian community we should cultivate sensitiveness to the sufferings of others. ' We have to learn afresh,' as the Message of the First General Assembly of the World Council of Churches puts it, '. . . to stand by the outcast, the prisoner and the refugee.' We need to drink very deeply of the springs of pity which are in Christ, if we, like Him, are going to be tenderhearted.

HUMBLEMINDED is interesting. Humility is a peculiarly biblical virtue. In classical Greek *tapeinos* ('humble-minded' here is *tapeinophron*) meant 'low' (e.g. of low-lying land) and, when used metaphorically, it was almost always in a bad sense—'base', 'ignoble', 'mean'.

Several streams flowed together to form the New Testament idea of humility. There was the historical experience of Israel: the people of God had not been prosperous and successful, but had suffered—the godly remnant most of all. The Hebrew word *ani* ('poor', 'meek') was one of the tributaries of the New Testament 'humble'. But there was something deeper than outward poverty in Israel's experience. This people, in contrast with the Greeks who were thoroughly anthropocentric in their thinking, was conscious that its whole life was 'before God'. They knew they had to deal with the living God, the Holy One, who is of purer eyes than to behold iniquity. They knew that the standard by which their life was judged was nothing less than the demands of His Law. Hence their sense of sin, their humility before God. Those, who judge themselves by their next-door neighbours, may feel quite satisfied: those, who know themselves to be judged by God's standards, must needs be humble. The Church entered into the experience of Israel, but Israel's insights were enlarged and transcended by the fulfilment of the Old Testament in Christ. The Christian has before his eyes the example of the terrific humility of Christ, the Son of God, who emptied Himself, taking the form of a slave, and who stooped to wash the feet of sinners and to die on the cross. How can the disciple disdain to be as his Lord? And that humility of Christ was for our sakes; the Christian experience is one of incalculable indebtedness to the love of God, and those who are conscious of a debt they cannot ever repay cannot help but be humble.

So there came about this 'transvaluation of values', and the word *tapeinos,* though occasionally used in the New Testament in a bad sense (e.g. Col. 2.18, 23), became a characteristic Christian word. Humblemindedness is an essential characteristic of those who belong to Him, who said that He was 'lowly (*tapeinos*) in heart'. There is one other thing, that should be noted about 'humbleminded', and that is the eschatological[1] promise that attaches to it: as Christ was humbled for a season but is now exalted, so too the Christian, humbling himself now, may look forward to sharing hereafter in his Lord's glory (cf. Matt. 23.12).

Lastly, NOT RENDERING EVIL FOR EVIL, OR REVILING FOR REVILING; BUT CONTRARIWISE BLESSING (cf. Luke 6. 27f.). Our natural instinct is to want to get even with those who hurt us, to give as good as we get, or like Lamech (Gen. 4.23f.) to have our own back—with interest. And, if we do not, we feel humiliated. What is here required of us is quite unnatural to us.

And, whether we ask the question, 'Why should we try to follow this way that is so contrary to our natural instincts and the ways of the world?' or the question, 'How are we to get the necessary strength to walk in it?' the Apostle has the answer ready for us: FOR HEREUNTO WERE YE CALLED, THAT YE SHOULD INHERIT A BLESSING. The divine blessing bestowed already in Christ and the inheritance God has in store for us—these are both the reason for the Christian life and the strength for it. 'Freely ye received, freely give', Jesus said to His disciples (Matt. 10.8). Both the motive and the dynamic lie in the divine gift. The secret is to look more and more steadily on the blessing already bestowed and the blessing in store for us. From that contemplation springs the deepening sense of gratitude, which is the reason and dynamic of the Christian ethic.

Finally, in accordance with his custom, the writer clinches the matter with a quotation from the Old Testament—from Ps. 34.

FOR,
HE THAT WOULD LOVE LIFE,
AND SEE GOOD DAYS,
LET HIM REFRAIN HIS TONGUE FROM EVIL,
AND HIS LIPS THAT THEY SPEAK NO GUILE:
AND LET HIM TURN AWAY FROM EVIL, AND DO GOOD;
LET HIM SEEK PEACE, AND PURSUE IT.
FOR THE EYES OF THE LORD ARE UPON THE RIGHTEOUS,

[1] For the meaning of 'eschatological' see note on p. 18.

AND HIS EARS UNTO THEIR SUPPLICATION:
BUT THE FACE OF THE LORD IS UPON THEM THAT DO EVIL.

The rough Greek of the LXX version has here been considerably improved (the work of Silvanus, no doubt), and a Christian turn has been given to it. The reference in the first words is no longer to length of life in this world and prosperity and happiness here; but to eternal life laid hold on here but to be fully enjoyed hereafter. The 'good days' refer to the inheritance in store for us. The appeal is to those, who really desire here and now to set their hearts on the life that is life indeed and hereafter to enter upon their inheritance. Perhaps the word 'love' which has been moved from the position it had in the LXX version is also meant to suggest a contrast with that hating life, of which we hear in Eccl. 2.17: the 'men of the world, whose portion is in this life' very often become bored with its pleasures and are frustrated and disillusioned; but those who seek eternal life have a zest that never falters.

Interpreted in the light of the Gospel, the words of the Psalm sum up simply and directly the way of life Peter has been describing. At the same time they emphasize the fact that the way of true happiness can only be that way that is in accordance with God's will. There is a real sense in which the stars in their courses always fight against the Siseras; for, the world having been made by God, all things are ultimately against us, so long as we try to by-pass Him. And, on the other hand, if we love God, He works with us in all things for our good.

CHAPTER TEN

BUT AND IF YE SHOULD SUFFER

(3.13-4.6)

ND WHO IS HE THAT WILL HARM YOU. . . ? takes up
the last phrase of the preceding section. The connection of thought is clearer in the original, as the
Greek words translated 'evil' (in 3.12) and 'he that will
harm' are from the same root (*kaka* and *kakoson*). The
Apostle realizes that his mention of 'them that do evil'
will quite probably send a cold shiver down the backs of
those whom he is addressing—for they would think of the
persecution they dreaded. So he quickly anticipates their
fears with his rhetorical question. And we may take what
he says to heart ourselves; for fear is a perennial problem.
If we do not have to fear persecution, there is still fear of
illness, of bereavement, of failure, of getting old, of losing
one's figure, of the next war, and so on. Peter's rhetorical
question expects the answer 'Nobody!' What it amounts
to is that there is nothing that can really hurt you, really do
you evil, provided . . . He does not say that you will never
have to suffer (the next sentence indicates that you may),
but that even suffering and death will be powerless really to
harm you, IF YE BE ZEALOUS OF THAT WHICH IS GOOD, i.e.
if you are out for the right thing ('that which is good') and
if you are really out for it whole-heartedly ('zealous'). On
the other hand, if your life is set in the wrong direction, if
what you really desire is but the passing pleasures of this
world, or if your love for God is only half-hearted, then
you will indeed be harmed; but those who seek the kingdom
of God and seek it with their whole heart, though not beyond the reach of suffering, are beyond the reach of harm.

The word 'zealous' (literally 'zealots') indicates that
whole-heartedness and singleness of purpose, which are

the mark of the Christian (cf. Matt. 6.19ff.). It is possible
that there is a reference to the Jewish party of the Zealots,[1]
those fanatical nationalists, whose fervent but misguided
zeal was to be one of the contributing causes of the fatal
Jewish War (A.D. 66-70). If so, it is like someone saying
to-day that Christians ought to take a leaf out of the book
of the Communists and be as whole-hearted and self-
sacrificing in their loyalty to Christ as Communists are in
their loyalty to 'the cause'.

Sufferings may indeed come—BUT AND IF YE SHOULD
SUFFER . . . It is the suffering of persecution that is
especially meant, but the Greek optative mood used here
and in verse 17 ('should so will') would seem to indicate a
possibility that in the author's judgment is somewhat remote
as far as the majority of those who are addressed is concerned. It suggests a different situation from that implied
by 4.12ff. The discrepancy is easily understandable, if
1.3-4.11 was composed earlier and then incorporated into a
letter called forth by the circumstances reflected in 4.12ff.
(cf. Chapter I).

Most of the sufferings that come to us are neutral in the
sense that they come to us as men, not as Christians particularly; and of course the Gospel should help us to face them
bravely. But sometimes we may have to suffer because we
are Christians—FOR RIGHTEOUSNESS' SAKE—and, when that
happens, says Peter, BLESSED ARE YE, you are to be con-
gratulated on your high privilege. For such suffering marks
a man out as an heir of the kingdom of God. It is bright
with promise. St. Peter doubtless had in mind the saying
of Christ recorded in Matt. 5.10.

The next words—AND FEAR NOT THEIR FEAR, NEITHER BE
TROUBLED; BUT SANCTIFY IN YOUR HEARTS CHRIST AS LORD—
are based on the LXX version of Isa. 8.12f., where the
R.V. has 'Say ye not, A conspiracy, concerning all whereof
this people shall say, A conspiracy; neither fear ye their
fear, nor be in dread thereof. The Lord of hosts, him shall
ye sanctify; and let him be your fear, and let him be your
dread'. The prophet and his disciples are warned not to
conform to the ideas of the people, nor to fear what the

[1] For the Zealots cf. Luke 6.15, Acts 1.13, Matt. 10.4, Mark
3.18 R.V. margin.

people are afraid of, but to fear the Lord God alone. As used here in 1 Peter, the words 'fear not their fear' (literally, 'fear not the fear of them') mean not 'do not fear what they fear', but 'do not fear them' (i.e. your possible persecutors). Christians must let the true fear—the fear of Christ their Lord—banish all false fears from their hearts. Other fears are unworthy and sordid; 'the fear of the Lord is clean'. The best way to be rid of craven fears is to have one's heart filled with the right fear of Christ. That was how Daniel Cargill, the Covenanter, could exclaim, with his foot on the gallows ladder, 'Lord knows I go up this ladder with less fear and perturbation than ever I entered a pulpit to preach.'

To sanctify Christ as Lord will involve BEING READY ALWAYS TO GIVE ANSWER TO EVERY MAN THAT ASKETH YOU A REASON CONCERNING THE HOPE THAT IS IN YOU. 'To give answer' could refer to a defence in court or equally well to answering in an informal conversation. In either circumstance a Christian must be ready to confess His Lord. 'A reason concerning' means 'a rational and intelligible account of'. That is something we can scarcely hope to be able to give, unless we have been at pains to understand the Gospel (cf. 1.13—'girding up the loins of your mind'). Mark 13.11 does not mean that Jesus approves of intellectual laziness! Peter's words put a question to us about our own preparedness. 'That is in you' could mean 'that inspires the Christian community' (collective), but more probably refers to the individual—'that is in your hearts'. But the answer is to be given with quiet dignity, not in a provocative or aggressive spirit—YET WITH MEEKNESS AND FEAR, i.e. with gentleness and courtesy towards those to whom it is addressed and with reverence for Him about whom we are speaking. The 'fear' is fear of God, not of those whom we have to answer. We are not to adopt a truculent attitude or to show contempt for our questioners, but to follow the pattern of Christ's quiet and dignified bearing before His judges and accusers, HAVING (or 'maintaining') A GOOD CONSCIENCE; THAT WHEREIN YE ARE SPOKEN AGAINST, THEY MAY BE PUT TO SHAME WHO REVILE YOUR GOOD MANNER OF LIFE IN CHRIST. Such a bearing, free alike from craven fear and from anger and resentment, and confirmed and supported by a truly Christian life, will put your slanderers to shame. But even if it should not have this desired effect, it would still be intrinsically preferable; FOR IT IS BETTER, IF THE WILL OF GOD SHOULD SO WILL (i.e. should will that you should suffer), THAT YE SUFFER FOR WELL-DOING THAN FOR EVIL-DOING. Cf. 2.20.

The remaining verses of this section (to 4.6) are without doubt the most difficult part of the letter. On a quick reading two sentences will probably strike us as specially perplexing—3.19f. and 4.6; 3.21 is also difficult, and so is 4.1. But, before we attempt to deal with particular problems, we had better try to get a general idea of the argument. Otherwise we shall be in grave danger of missing the wood for the trees. The core of the first half of the passage (3.18-22) is the first part of verse 18 ('Because . . . to God'), which brings forward a reason in support of the statement just made in verse 17 that, if they must suffer, it is better for them to suffer for well-doing than for evil-doing. Peter appeals to Christ's Passion—BECAUSE CHRIST ALSO SUFFERED. . . . He thinks of it as an example to be followed: that is the force of the 'also'. But the way in which he speaks of it makes it abundantly clear that for him its exemplary value by no means exhausts its significance. It is far more than a pattern for us to copy. The deeper meaning of the cross is indicated in this verse, as we shall see. But Peter knows that Christ's sufferings cannot be rightly understood unless they are seen in the light of His victory. So the sequel to the Passion is set forth in the remaining verses of the chapter. At the same time a reference to Baptism is introduced, which, though the manner of its introduction appears to be quite casual (suggested by the mention of Noah and the Ark), is nevertheless significant for the interpretation of the following verses. The core of 4.1-6 is 4.1f. It picks up the argument of 3.18 —but with the additional meaning that the reference to Baptism has given it—and reiterates the moral exhortation, though in more general terms. Verses 3-6 are added in support of what has been said in 1 and 2.

We must now look at this passage a little more closely. First there is what Peter has here to say about the cross. Christ suffered, he tells us, FOR SINS (cf. 1 Cor. 15.3, Gal.

1.4, Heb. 10.12). The cross was God's method of dealing
with man's sin. Christ died in order to take away the sin
of the world. His death was ONCE for all, utterly unique
and utterly conclusive. Compare Rom. 6.9f., Heb. 7.27,
9.12, 26, 28, 10.10, and the words of the Communion Service in the Book of Common Prayer—'who made there (by
his one oblation of himself once offered) a full, perfect and
sufficient sacrifice, oblation and satisfaction for the sins
of the whole world'. His death was vicarious; He died in
our place, THE RIGHTEOUS FOR THE UNRIGHTEOUS. 'He was
wounded for our transgressions . . . The Lord hath laid
on him the iniquity of us all.' The purpose of His death
WAS THAT HE MIGHT BRING US TO GOD. One could hardly
express the meaning of the cross better than these simple
words express it. We may compare Rom. 5.2 and Eph.
2.18, and also John 14.6.

The next phrase—BEING PUT TO DEATH IN THE FLESH, BUT
QUICKENED IN THE SPIRIT—is not, as it might seem, a contradiction of the biblical doctrine of the resurrection of the
body; rather it means that, while the body of Christ that
was crucified was subject to the frailty and limitations of
an ordinary human body, the body that was raised up,
though it bore the scars of His death, is no longer subject
to such limitations (e.g. He passed through closed doors
according to John 20.19, 26), but is a spiritual body. We
may compare the use of 'flesh' and 'spirit' in 1 Tim.
3.16 and also the general idea of 1 Cor. 15.42ff. (especially
the first part of verse 44).

It was in this condition of freedom from the limitations
of the days of His flesh IN WHICH ALSO[1] HE WENT AND
PREACHED UNTO THE SPIRITS IN PRISON, WHICH AFORETIME
WERE DISOBEDIENT, WHEN THE LONGSUFFERING OF GOD
WAITED IN THE DAYS OF NOAH, WHILE THE ARK WAS A PRE-
PARING. . . . Who are these 'spirits in prison'? Some
commentators take them to be the fallen angels, those
'sons of God', of whose misconduct we hear in Gen. 6.
The word 'spirit' is sometimes used in the Bible of angelic

[1] We may safely reject Rendel Harris' ingenious conjectural
emendation of the text, which introduces Enoch as the subject of
'went and preached', although Moffatt and others accepted it. A
reference to Enoch would be quite irrelevant here.

beings, and there was a tradition that disobedient angels
had been imprisoned by God (cf. 2 Peter 2.4, Jude 6.).
Selwyn accepts this view and understands *ekeryxen* (which
the R.V. renders 'preached') to mean not that He preached
the Gospel to them but that He made proclamation to
them of the approaching end of their power as a result of
His victory.   On the whole it seems more satisfactory to
take *ekeryxen* in its normal New Testament sense and to
understand by 'the spirits in prison' the generation of mankind that perished in the Flood.   These would be mentioned as being generally regarded as the most notorious
and abandoned of sinners: if there was hope for them, then
none could be beyond the reach of Christ's saving power.
Perhaps the author was also influenced in his choice of
these particular sinners by the thought that the mention
of Noah and the ark would afford him a convenient way of
introducing the subject of Baptism?

The suggestion that 'went and preached' refers to a
preaching by Christ before His incarnation and through the
lips of Noah to those, who now are in prison, but at the
time of this preaching were still alive, is far-fetched.   The
natural reference is to an activity of Christ after His death
—presumably in the interval between His death and resurrection.   (Or could it be an action of the risen Christ?)
The idea of a descent of Christ into Hades is found elsewhere in the New Testament: it is quite false to the facts
to imagine that the idea is dependent solely on this passage,
as some have done (cf. Acts 2.27, 31, Rom. 10.6-8, Eph.
4.8-10).   The further idea that Christ's saving work reached
those who were dead is to be found in John 5.25-29 (also
Matt. 27.52f.?).   Perhaps this is also the meaning of 'he
led captivity captive' in Eph. 4.8.   We cannot enter here
upon a long discussion of this subject, about which a vast
amount has been written; though something must be said
about it.   To talk about 'the fantastic dream of a descent
of Christ into Hades' and to declare that 'it is nothing else
than the appropriation, and the application to Christ, of a
fragment of the redemption-mythology of the Oriental re-
ligions, best known to us in the ancient story of the Descent
of Ishtar to the underworld, and reflected also in a number
of Greek myths (Orpheus and Eurydice, Heracles and

Alcestis, the story of Persephone, etc.); it is rooted in old vegetation- and sun-myths ', as Beare does, seems to the present writer to be an example of thinking one knows the answer, when in reality one does not. This is one of those texts, which keep us guessing. We cannot trace Christ's story between the moment of His death and ' the first day of the week . . . early, while it was yet dark '. This verse indicates that that interval was not without significance, and that in it, as at other times, Jesus Christ was active as the Saviour of the world, and that the scope of His saving activity is such that we dare set no limits to it. The best thing is to realize that we encounter here a mystery, which is still a secret from us, and reverently to accept the hint— for a hint is all that is given to us—and thank God that the reach of Christ's saving activity is not to be limited by our human desire to get things neat and tidy in pigeon-holes of our choosing.

The passage continues: WHEREIN FEW, THAT IS, EIGHT SOULS, WERE SAVED THROUGH WATER: WHICH ALSO AFTER A TRUE LIKENESS DOTH NOW SAVE YOU, EVEN BAPTISM, NOT THE PUTTING AWAY OF THE FILTH OF THE FLESH, BUT THE INTERROGATION OF A GOOD CONSCIENCE TOWARD GOD, THROUGH THE RESURRECTION OF JESUS CHRIST. . . . If we leave aside for the moment the words ' not the putting away . . . toward God ', which are a parenthesis, the general sense of the rest is clear. A comparison is indicated between the water of the Flood and the water of Baptism, between Noah and his seven companions in the ark and the Christians whom Peter is addressing, and between Noah's being saved and their being saved. Even the contrast between the fewness of those in the ark and the multitudes of contemporary mankind that perished in the Flood has its counterpart in the smallness of the Church in comparison with the pagan world. The preposition ' through ' before ' water ' was presumably chosen, because it could equally well have a local or an instrumental sense, and so would make easier the transition to Baptism. The little company in the ark were saved through water, in the sense that they were brought safely through the element which was destroying others; it is also true that in a sense water was the means of their safety, for it bore the ark. In the case of Baptism the water is the means of salvation, though it is also true that it symbolizes the death into which we are buried with Christ (Rom. 6.4), through which we are brought to new life with the risen Christ. The Greek word, which the R.V. renders by 'after a true likeness', is *antitypon*—a word that belongs to the typological interpretation of the Scriptures that was current in the early Church, according to which persons, things and events of the Old Dispensation were regarded as types or foreshadowings of persons, things and events of the New (cf. Matt. 2.15, 17, 12.40, 1 Cor. 9.9f., 10.1ff., Gal. 4.24ff., etc.). The 'antitype' is the reality foreshadowed by the type. It is difficult to be quite certain whether the Greek word *antitypon* here is to be construed closely with 'which' (i.e. water) or with 'you'; we need not concern ourselves here with these grammatical complications, seeing that the general sense will be the same anyway. On the whole it seems best to follow Selwyn in taking *antitypon* as a substantive in apposition to 'you'. He renders the Greek thus: 'And water now saves you too, who are the antitype of Noah and his company, namely the water of Baptism. . . .' The word 'now', as it stands in the Epistle, simply denotes the time of the New Dispensation, but, if we are right in thinking this part was originally a sermon at a baptismal service, its original significance was more emphatic.

But the sacrament of Baptism can be misunderstood; so the Apostle seeks to guard against possible misunderstandings. It is not some property of the water that makes the sacrament effective; the efficacy of the sacrament originates in that which it signifies. The water of Baptism 'saves . . . through the resurrection of Jesus Christ'—by applying to the person baptized the benefits of Christ's death and resurrection. The saving power is the resurrection of Christ. It is similarly to guard against possible misunderstanding that the parenthesis is introduced in the middle of verse 21. Baptism is not a mere cleansing of the body, but 'the interrogation of a good conscience toward God'. The second half of the parenthesis is something of a riddle. The missing clue is the Greek word *eperotema,* the exact significance of which is uncertain. 'Question', 'enquiry', would be the natural meaning, but that does not make very good sense (unless conceivably there is a reference to the solemn questions put to the candidate for Baptism? or could the word include both the question and the response?); it might perhaps mean 'request' or 'prayer' (though the verb *eperotao* means to ask a question rather than ask a request), in which case the phrase might mean either 'a prayer to God for a good conscience, i.e. for forgiveness' or ' a prayer to God proceeding from a good conscience'.   Another possible meaning—and this seems to be most satisfactory—is 'pledge'.   There is some evidence in papyri for the word being used for the formal question and consent which sealed a contract.   The whole phrase might then mean either 'a pledge to God to maintain a good conscience' (which could be connected with the promise to renounce the world, the flesh and the devil) or 'a pledge proceeding from a good conscience' or more probably 'a pledge of a good conscience toward God', i.e. Baptism is a pledge or assurance or earnest of God's forgiveness of sins.   This would seem to be the best sense, but we must admit that we are not certain that *eperotema* has yielded its secret.

Verse 22 completes the picture of Christ's victory, the context and ground of Baptism and the context of the sufferings of Christ mentioned in verse 18—WHO IS ON THE RIGHT HAND OF GOD, HAVING GONE INTO HEAVEN; ANGELS AND AUTHORITIES AND POWERS BEING MADE SUBJECT UNTO HIM.

The first words of chapter 4—FORASMUCH THEN AS CHRIST SUFFERED IN THE FLESH—take up again the thought of 3.18. The 'then' is resumptive. ARM YE YOURSELVES ALSO WITH THE SAME MIND appears at first sight to mean the same as the R.V. translation of Phil. 2.5 ('Have this mind in you, which was also in Christ Jesus') and to be an exhortation to put on as armour that same spirit of gentleness and patience in suffering that Jesus displayed.   This sounds all right, until we go on to the next sentence: FOR HE THAT HATH SUFFERED IN THE FLESH HATH CEASED FROM SIN.   If we understand 'the same mind' as we have done above, we shall have to take this next sentence to mean that suffering patiently and meekly borne cleanses the sufferer.   This is no doubt quite true; but it does not fit in very well in this context, and anyway 'has ceased from sin' is a most extravagant way of stating it. Suffering borne in a Christlike spirit certainly has a cleansing effect, but that is not the same as saying that it frees a man from sin, so that he sins no more. Beare is surely on the right track here, when he compares Rom. 6.7—'For he that hath died is justified from sin' and interprets in the light of what Paul says about Baptism in that chapter. Those who have been baptized have been baptized into Christ's death and have been buried with Him through Baptism; they have therefore died to sin. There is no need, however, to conclude that we have here an instance of borrowing from Paul; for it is likely that both Apostles are making use of a proverbial expression, whose original meaning was probably simply 'Death pays all debts', or possibly of a rabbinic maxim to the effect that once dead a man is free from the Law and the Commandments. Moreover, Paul seems to imply (Rom. 6.3) that what he is saying about Baptism was something generally accepted. So we conclude that 'the same mind' does not mean 'the same spirit as that which Christ displayed', but rather 'the knowledge that you have suffered (died) with Christ through Baptism, that your old life has been crucified with Him, and that now you share His risen life'. (We may compare Rom. 6.10f.); and that 'he that hath suffered in the flesh hath ceased from sin' means 'the man who has through Baptism been made to share in Christ's death has died to sin'.[1]

But justification, the fact that in God's sight our sinful life has been buried and is a thing of the past and that now Christ's risen life is our real life, demands that we should strive to become in our actual living what we already are in God's sight. So Peter goes on to add what is the purpose for which they must 'arm' themselves—THAT YE NO LONGER SHOULD LIVE THE REST OF YOUR TIME IN THE FLESH TO THE LUSTS OF MEN, BUT TO THE WILL OF GOD. Again we may compare the words of the letter to the Romans: 'We who died to sin, how shall we any longer live therein?' (Rom. 6.2). FOR THE TIME PAST MAY SUFFICE TO HAVE WROUGHT THE DESIRE OF THE GENTILES, AND TO HAVE WALKED IN

[1] It is possible that we should translate *hoti* in 4.1, not 'for' as R.V. does, but 'that', and take closely with 'the same mind'—thus 'arm yourselves also with this same thought, namely that . . .'

LASCIVIOUSNESS, LUSTS, WINEBIBBINGS, REVELLINGS, CAR-
OUSINGS, AND ABOMINABLE IDOLATRIES. Long enough of
this short life has been wasted already. What remains is
only a fragment; but at all events let that which remains
be spent in obedience to God. The three perfect tenses in
the Greek ('past', 'to have wrought', and 'to have walked')
emphasize the thought that these things are indeed things
of the past, a closed chapter. These words would have been
especially appropriate and impressive, if addressed originally to those who had just been baptized; for everything
about Baptism in the early Church (as also on the mission
field to-day) emphasized its significance as the decisive
turning-point in a man's life, the break with the heathen
past.

It was only natural that those who remained pagans
should take it ill that people who had been their companions
in the old ways should no longer conform to the familiar
pattern of pagan life. WHEREIN THEY THINK IT STRANGE
THAT YE RUN NOT WITH THEM INTO THE SAME EXCESS OF
RIOT, SPEAKING EVIL OF YOU. That is still a common experience of those who take the decisive step and turn from
a pagan, secular way of life, to the Christian pilgrimage.
Such resentment is to be expected.

But, if Christians are liable to have to face the resentful
criticism and spite of those who take offence at their good
life, these critics will have to face what is much more fear-
ful—the judgment-seat of Christ, the appointed Judge of
both living and dead. WHO SHALL GIVE ACCOUNT TO HIM
THAT IS READY TO JUDGE THE QUICK AND THE DEAD. The
phrase 'the quick and the dead' is a stereotyped phrase in
connection with judgment, and is quite likely used here
automatically. If not, the point would be that even death
will not remove them from the reach of judgment. This
mention of 'the dead' suggests a further thought, which is
expressed in the next verse. FOR UNTO THIS END WAS THE
GOSPEL PREACHED EVEN TO THE DEAD, THAT THEY MIGHT
BE JUDGED ACCORDING TO MEN IN THE FLESH, BUT LIVE
ACCORDING TO GOD IN THE SPIRIT. Some seek to explain this
by reference to the question raised by the Thessalonians
and answered in 1 Thess. 4.13ff., and take 'the dead' to
mean those Christians, who heard the Gospel during their

lifetime, but have since died—before the Lord's return. Others have taken 'the dead' to mean the spiritually dead. But the most natural interpretation is surely to connect it with 3.19, and to understand a reference to 'the spirits in prison'. Though 'that they might be judged' and 'live' are co-ordinate grammatically, it is best to take the former as subordinate to the latter in thought, so that the meaning will be: 'in order that, though they have died, as all men must (death itself being regarded as God's judgment), they might nevertheless live by God's power in the spirit'. In the opinion of men the dead have had their judgment; but the Good News has been preached even among them, in order that those who respond to it might live eternally. For 'in the spirit' cf. what was said above on 3.18. Two different Greek words are used, where R.V. has the same word 'live' (in verses 2 and 6); the word used in verse 2 denotes the transitory life of this earthly existence; the other word denotes in the New Testament eternal life. Such eternal life is 'according to God', a divine gift, not a human possibility.

CHAPTER ELEVEN

THE END OF ALL THINGS IS AT HAND

(4.7-11)

ERHAPS someone might imagine that the judgment referred to in verse 5 is so far away in the dim and hazy distance that it could not possibly have any practical significance for us. The striking sentence with which this new section begins is calculated to disturb any such complacent illusions. BUT THE END OF ALL THINGS IS AT HAND. It tells us two things. The first is that this ambiguous world is not going on in its ambiguity for ever. It will come to an end. The curtain will one day fall. Heaven and earth will pass away. It will be the end—both in the sense of termination and in the sense of consummation. It will be the end, inasmuch as history will then be over and done with, its course brought to a stop. But the end is also the goal, the meaning of history, the thing which gives significance to its whole course. It is the last day, which gives meaningfulness to all our days. But, when we say that the end is the goal of history, we must not make the mistake of thinking that that implies that it is simply the final self-fulfilment of the life of this world, the final and complete stage of this world's self-expression. It is not the consummation of all things in that sense. The new order is not a part of the historical process, it does not evolve from the present order; on the contrary, it is the breaking in of that which is outside and beyond history, the replacing, not the self-fulfilment, of this order. The whole Bible bears witness to this end of all things. And it tells us that the end is not something impersonal, not a mere cosmic catastrophe, but the coming again in glory of Him who once came in humility. Because that is so, the message of the end is good news.

The other thing that Peter's striking sentence tells us is that the end is near. This nearness of the end is part of the New Testament's witness. 'The night is far spent, and the day is at hand,' writes Paul to the Romans. 'Little children, it is the last hour,' says the First Epistle of John (2.18). And the last book of the Bible closes with the assurance by the glorified Christ, 'Yea, I come quickly', and the answering prayer of the waiting Church, 'Amen: come, Lord Jesus' (Rev. 22.20). But it is now almost nineteen hundred years since the New Testament books were written, and the end has not yet come. Does it mean that the early Church was mistaken, that our Lord Himself was mistaken? Has history proved Him to have been wrong?

The answer is 'No!'—for to say that the end is near is not the exact equivalent of saying that it is going to happen within a few years. The end is near in a much more radical sense than that. According to the New Testament 'the last days' have already begun. They began with the Incarnation. The supreme event of history has already taken place, that event in which the meaning of history (which is outside and beyond history) did actually become for a while a part of history. That was the climax, the final chapter; all subsequent history is but epilogue,[1] a period, in which men have opportunity to come to terms with the meaning of history and of their lives, as it has been revealed in history. So in this letter Peter has already spoken of the time of Christ's Incarnation as 'the end of the times' (1.20). We may compare Acts 2.16f., where Peter in his Pentecost Day Sermon says that Joel's prophecy of the last days has been fulfilled (cf. also Heb. 1.2, 9.26). The epilogue may soon end or it may go on for a very long time; but the end is all the time near, threatening, pressing upon this world, so to speak. The end is near, because this world is a conquered world. Christ has already won the decisive battle, and what remains of the war is merely the last skirmishing of a beaten foe. The end is near, because it is the meaning of the present, and every historical crisis is a kind of dress rehearsal of the end. The very frustrations and calamities of this

[1] Cf. 'The Church, Russia and the West', a stimulating article by Martin Wight, in The Ecumenical Review, I.1.

world are signs, and even pledges, of the end; for they announce plainly the corruption and impermanence of this world, they announce its passing away, and so—for the eye of faith—they are pointers to the end, so that Jesus can say: 'When these things begin to come to pass, look up, and lift up your heads; because your redemption draweth nigh' (Luke 21.28). And for each one of us the end is as near as death, which for the individual effects what might be called a telescoping of the last days.

The rest of the section consists of the conclusions, which St. Peter draws from this imminence of the end. The first is: BE YE THEREFORE OF SOUND MIND. The nearness of the end is no excuse for losing our mental or moral balance. We are not to throw up our jobs, as some of the Thessalonians apparently did. We are not to give way to panic, undue excitement or emotionalism, but rather to 'study to be quiet and to do our own business'. The sound mind is equally far removed from the worldliness and unbelief of those who think to explain away the promise of Christ's coming again and from the fanaticism and sensationalism of those who would fain predict the hour of it and the manner. The second conclusion is closely related to the first: AND BE SOBER UNTO PRAYER. Sobriety in the literal sense is no doubt part of what is intended, as verse 3 indicates; but the word also denotes here the sobriety of judgment of those who see the things of this life in true proportion because they see them in the light of eternity. To be sober unto prayer means avoiding all that would fuddle the mind, impair alertness, warp the vision and obstruct communion with God, whether intemperance of the body or preoccupation with the cares of the world and the deceitfulness of riches or smug self-righteousness or whatever else it may be. We are to take heed, watch and pray, for we know not when the time is (Mark 13.33).

The third conclusion—and he gives it the pre-eminence —is: ABOVE ALL THINGS BEING FERVENT IN YOUR LOVE AMONG YOURSELVES. We may compare the way in which St. Paul also connects the duty of love with the Advent hope (Rom. 13.8, 11). The chief way in which we are to show ourselves children, not of the darkness of this present world, but of God's new day, is by loving one another—and that energetically and persistently, in face of all discouragements. 'Fervently' gives perhaps a wrong nuance; for it might suggest that the emphasis is on warmth of emotion, whereas the Greek word it represents (used in the New Testament also in 1.22, Luke 22.44, Acts 12.5) suggests rather the taut muscle of strenuous and sustained effort, as of an athlete. Its root idea is 'stretching'. Xenophon uses the verb to describe a horse at full gallop. So 'strenuous' or 'persistent' would probably be a better rendering here. It suggests a certain toughness of love, love which endures. That love of the brethren, which is the badge of the Christian (John 13.35), is not just a matter of the emotions, whether warm feelings for the brethren in general or even for particular brothers, but involves the will and work and strenuous effort. It will lead to self-sacrificing service of them, which may well prove exacting, and it will have to be persistent in the face of all sorts of hindrances—including lack of appreciation on the part of the brothers concerned. It must have staying-power, like that of the runner in the long-distance race, for many will be the difficulties and discouragements.

The next words—FOR LOVE COVERETH A MULTITUDE OF SINS—are not quite clear. There are several possible meanings: (1) if your love for the brethren is real and strong, you will be ready to forgive them again and again; (2) if you love the brethren, then God will overlook the multitude of your sins (cf. Matt. 6.14f.); (3) God's love covers the multitude of your sins—therefore in gratitude to Him you must love strenuously. Prov. 10.12 is often assumed to underlie this, but the LXX text is quite different, and it is the LXX not the Hebrew from which the quotations in this letter are taken. At all events, the saying was proverbial in the early Church, though it was not always used in the same sense. One third-century writing attributes it to our Lord. The best sense is given here, if we adopt (1), though allowing for the possibility that (3) is also in the back of the writer's mind. In the earthly Church love must be very largely concerned with forgiveness, since we are all frail and sinful. We shall have to overlook much in one another; but, if the love which we have is really strong and strenuous, we shall forgive the multitude of our brethren's sins, knowing at the same time that we depend on God's forgiveness of the multitude of our sins. The use of the expression 'cover' in the sense of forgiveness derives from the Old Testament (e.g. Ps. 32.1).

St. Peter continues: USING HOSPITALITY ONE TO ANOTHER WITHOUT MURMURING. Here is a further conclusion from the nearness of the end or, if we prefer it, a way in which our strenuous love is to show itself. Compare Matt. 25.35, Rom. 12.13, 1 Tim. 3.2, Heb. 13.1f. The duties of hospitality, so important in the ancient world generally, had received a new and surpassing sanction from Christ—'I was a stranger, and ye took me in . . . Inasmuch as ye did it unto one of these my brethren, even these least, ye did it unto me.' Moreover, the missionary activity of the early Church was very largely dependent upon the hospitality of the brethren; for on the one hand, the Gospel was spread by travelling Christians, whether apostles and prophets or plain brethren, who had occasion to travel from place to place in the course of their business, and on the other hand, there were no church buildings for the first two hundred years or so and each local Church would have to meet in the house of one of the members (cf. Rom. 16.5, Philem. 2). Hospitality must often have suffered a big strain. It must often have been inconvenient and sometimes exasperating. Only those who lived the present in the light of eternity, and whose love had staying-power, would be able to be unfailingly hospitable, and that without murmuring. We shall not need very much imagination to translate this into modern terms and see its various applications for to-day!

The next verse reminds us of the truth, which should enable us to love and serve in whatever ways we can with humility and joy, and without murmuring. ACCORDING AS EACH HATH RECEIVED A GIFT, MINISTERING IT AMONG YOUR-SELVES, AS GOOD STEWARDS OF THE MANIFOLD GRACE OF GOD. Each member of the Church has received from God some particular endowment, some aptness or the where-withal for some particular service. It may be the gift of preaching, of the special qualities that are necessary for a sick-visitor or for teaching in the Sunday School or showing strangers to their seats or getting the church warm in time for the morning Service, or it may be having a room in one's house commodious enough to hold a study circle, or it may be the ability to help financially. The gifts differ widely, but they are all alike gifts from God. So we must not boast, as though they were our achievements (cf. 1 Cor. 4.7). And we have received them, not for our own private possession, but in trust for the whole Church—as stewards. So we are to minister them, each of us the particular gift entrusted to him, for the good of all. For the meaning of these gifts we may compare Rom. 12.3-8, 1 Cor. 12.-14. and also 1 Cor. 1.7, 7.7, 1 Tim. 4.14, 2 Tim. 1.6. Paul connects them particularly with the Holy Spirit—so much so that occasionally he uses the neuter plural of the adjective ' spiritual ' by itself to denote them (e.g. 1 Cor. 14.1). Though they are ultimately derived from God's grace, that is, God's love in action in Jesus Christ, they are mediated by the Holy Spirit. For the idea of stewardship we may compare Luke 12.42-48, 16.1-8, 1 Cor. 4.1f., Eph. 1.10, 3.2, 9, Col. 1.25, Tit. 1.7 (in the Eph. and Col. references see R.V. margin), and for the phrase ' good stewards of the manifold grace of God ' Eph. 3.2. It would seem best to take ' of the grace ' both in Eph. 3.2 and here as a subjective, rather than an objective, genitive; or, in other words, to understand the meaning to be that God's grace has called us to serve as stewards, not that God's grace is somehow the object of our stewardship (i.e. the thing with which our stewardship deals), as though it were something transferred into our power for us to manage and control. It is the gifts, ultimately derived from God's grace in Christ but mediated by the Spirit, which we manage as stewards, not the divine grace itself! (If on the other hand ' of the grace ' here really is an objective genitive, then ' grace ' is not used in its primary and characteristic Christian sense, but in a derived sense, and is more or less equivalent to the gifts.) God's grace is ' manifold ', as being the free personal activity of Him, whose resources of wisdom and power are unfathomable, whose love is altogether beyond our understanding, and whose ways are past our tracing out.

Peter now gives two examples of gifts. The first is the gift of preaching—IF ANY MAN SPEAKETH, SPEAKING AS IT

G

WERE ORACLES OF GOD. Does someone preach? If what he does is really preaching, then it is no human accomplishment, but a miracle. Preaching is God's Word. But the only words that the preacher can utter are human words, all of them broken and inadequate. Preaching only takes place when the Holy Spirit works a miracle and makes the broken human words become a real witness to the Word of God, themselves a living Word of God to the hearers. That is something which no preacher can 'lay on' or produce at will. He is dependent on the free decision of God. Therefore, when he has done everything that he can possibly do in the way of preparation—and there is no excuse for human slackness here!—he must still follow Augustine's advice and pray that God may *give* him His good Word into his mouth. To remember that is to be humble.

The second example is: IF ANY MAN MINISTERETH, MINISTERING AS OF THE STRENGTH WHICH GOD SUPPLIETH. 'Ministering' refers to the practical expression of love, e.g. feeding the hungry, caring for the sick, for the refugee, visiting the prisoner. Those who minister in the ways of practical service are to remember that they too are stewards, and that the wherewithal of their service, the physical strength to do it, the time and liberty, the resources, whether they are the gifts of the congregation or their own private substance, all these are God's gifts. It is God who furnishes abundantly the means of service. To remember this is to draw the sting from charity, the sense of patronizing and being patronized. The word translated 'supplieth' originally meant 'to lead a chorus' in the theatre, then 'to defray the expenses of bringing out a chorus at a public festival'. Hence it came to be used of providing supplies for an army or fleet, and so generally of equipping or furnishing, usually with the idea of abundance. So here it means that God provides for the welfare of His Church unstintingly.

Now finally we are told what is the goal and motive of all this: THAT IN ALL THINGS GOD MAY BE GLORIFIED THROUGH JESUS CHRIST. All is to be done to the glory of God, which is the true purpose of all the activities of Christians (cf. 2.5, Matt. 5.16). 'Through Jesus Christ' is added,

as Beare says, 'because all our relationships with Him are
mediated through His Son', or perhaps more particularly,
because all these activities of service and edification have
their source in Christ. The last words of the section are
a doxology: WHOSE IS THE GLORY AND THE DOMINION FOR
EVER AND EVER. AMEN.

CHAPTER TWELVE

THE FIERY TRIAL

(4.12-19)

IF the suggestion that 1.3-4.11 had already been used for another purpose is correct, then it is here that the material specially composed for the purpose of this letter begins (apart from the opening address, 1.1-2). What follows certainly seems to reflect a somewhat different situation from that reflected in 3.14ff. In the earlier passage persecution would seem to be still a comparatively remote possibility, while in the present section the fiery trial is apparently already beginning. The most likely explanation would seem to be that something has happened that has convinced these Christians in Asia Minor that the storm, which has for a long time been threatening and some warning drops of which they may already have felt, is now beginning in earnest. This situation would be the occasion of the letter being sent.

The ordeal of persecution is something that we in Britain have not experienced; but that must not blind us to the fact that during the last few decades in country after country the Church has become once more ' the Church under the cross '. The persecution of the Church in Germany under the Nazis is only one example out of many that could be named. The story of the persecution in the Roman Empire is familiar, and we need not enter into any description of it here; but we may allow these verses to deepen our sense of solidarity with our brethren, who are enduring persecution in other lands to-day. At the same time we may draw from them comfort and encouragement in the face of our less serious trials. The lions in the arena, the flames, the executioner's sword, the concentration-camp, the firing-squad—these we do not have to face; but even for some of us it is sometimes not an easy thing to be loyal to Christ in factory or office or barracks, while those of us,

whose lot is most sheltered, may at least be challenged
to contrast our own reluctance to bear small inconveni-
ences for the sake of Christ with the cost at which the
martyrs of the past and of our own days have confessed
Him.

BELOVED, THINK IT NOT STRANGE CONCERNING THE FIERY
TRIAL AMONG YOU, WHICH COMETH UPON YOU TO PROVE YOU,
AS THOUGH A STRANGE THING HAPPENED UNTO YOU: BUT IN-
SOMUCH AS YE ARE PARTAKERS OF CHRIST'S SUFFERINGS,
REJOICE; THAT AT THE REVELATION OF HIS GLORY ALSO YE
MAY REJOICE WITH EXCEEDING JOY. What does this tell us
about the ordeal of persecution? First, we are not to be
surprised at it. Here is something that is to be expected,
something that is characteristic of the life of the Church in
this world. Compare Matt. 5.11f., Mark 13.13, John 15.18-
20, 16.33, 1 John 3.13, etc. On the contrary, it would be
surprising if Christians were not persecuted; for their very
existence is an affront to human self-centredness, a reminder
of the absolute claims that God makes upon men's lives
and that so many want to ignore and forget. We may ask
ourselves whether perhaps our freedom from persecution
and even from unpopularity is not solely due to the good-
humoured, tolerant spirit of our non-Christian countrymen,
but also in part the result of our not taking Christ and His
claims upon us too seriously. Were we more uncom-
promisingly and consistently Christian, might it be otherwise?

The second thing that this passage says is that the fiery
trial is a testing, whereby the reality or unreality of our
faith is made manifest. It 'cometh upon you to prove you'.
Those whose Christianity is not real vanish from the ranks
at the approach of danger.

The third thing is that it is a sharing in Christ's sufferings.
The disciple is called to take up his cross and follow his
Master. But this sharing is a two-way sharing. We share
in His sufferings, and He shares in ours. We share His
reproach, and, when we are in the burning fiery furnace, He
walks with us amid the flames, or when the Church is
lashed by the storm, and winds and waves are contrary,
His disciples may expect Him to come to them at the dark-
est hour walking upon the waters.

The fourth thing, which is inseparable from the third, is that the fiery trial is a cause for joy. To share Christ's shame is a glorious privilege, to have His fellowship—though it be in the midst of the flames—is to have fullness of joy, and to partake of His humiliation in this world is the pledge of participation in His glory in the world to come.

This last point is further emphasized in the following words: IF YE ARE REPROACHED FOR THE NAME OF CHRIST, BLESSED ARE YE (cf. Matt. 5.11f., Acts 5.41, Phil. 1.29); BECAUSE THE SPIRIT OF GLORY AND THE SPIRIT OF GOD RESTETH UPON YOU. The first 'Spirit' is printed in italics in the R.V., which means that it has no equivalent in the original. The Greek text means literally, 'the of (the) glory and the Spirit of God'. It is possible that the curious expression, 'the of the glory', denotes the Shekinah, the visible brightness or glory that was the sign of God's presence (cf. Exod. 16.7, 24.16, 29.43, 40.34, Num. 14.10, 1 Kings 8.10f., Isa. 6.1ff., Ezek. 1.28, Haggai 2.7, etc., and in the New Testament Luke 2.9, Matt. 17.5, Rom. 9.4, etc.), as Selwyn thinks. The meaning would then be that the bright visible glory, which had been the sign of God's presence with His people in the desert and had been seen over the Tabernacle and had filled the Temple and which had overshadowed the mount of Transfiguration, rests with the Holy Spirit on the suffering Church under the cross. But perhaps it is more natural to translate these words: 'the Spirit of glory and of God'. The meaning is then that God's Holy Spirit, who Himself is glorious and also the source of glory and whose presence is the pledge of future glory (cf. the Pauline phrase, 'the earnest of the Spirit'), rests and abides upon the persecuted Church.

To guard against possible misunderstanding, verse 15 is added: FOR LET NONE OF YOU SUFFER AS A MURDERER, OR A THIEF, OR AN EVIL-DOER, OR AS A MEDDLER IN OTHER MEN'S MATTERS. What was said in the preceding verse had reference to sufferings incurred for Christ's sake, not to those incurred by wrong-doing (cf. 2.20). The first two things —murderer, thief—are obvious. The third would seem to be a general term to cover other wrong-doing punishable by law. So far the list would command immediate assent.

There is clearly nothing creditable in suffering a punishment which one has deserved by plain wrong-doing. That is not martyrdom. The fourth term is a little perplexing. The Greek word represented by 'a meddler in other men's matters' occurs only here in the New Testament, and outside it only in Dionysius the Areopagite, who uses it of a bishop interfering in another bishop's territory. Some scholars, thinking that this word too must denote someone whose action would be punishable by law, suggest the meaning 'revolutionary', but there is no real evidence for this. As a matter of fact, it is possible that the repetition of 'as' here (it is not repeated before the two preceding terms) may reflect a conscious transition to a different category. At any rate, it is best to follow the R.V. rendering, which gives the natural sense of the compound. There is possibly a trace of humour in introducing the busybody into this disreputable list. Peter is warning his readers against drawing upon themselves unpopularity and persecution by unnecessary interference in their neighbours' affairs or by interference that is necessary but is made in an officious and provocative manner. It is a warning that is still timely. We have no right to regard ourselves as martyrs, when the unpopularity or even persecution which we encounter, is the result either of an officious and unnecessary interference on our part or of a right stand taken in a provocative or self-righteous manner. We may well allow God's Word to question us about the occasions and the spirit and manner of some of our protests and crusades. Do we sometimes make ourselves unpopular for the wrong things, ostentatiously and provocatively straining out gnats, while at the same time quietly and unprotestingly swallowing camels or by doing that which is right in the wrong manner? Do we sometimes in those matters, in which God's Word leaves each man free to decide for himself what is expedient, try to bind other men's consciences with our own scruples and to replace the freedom for which Christ set us free by a new legalism of our own devising? Do we sometimes refuse to acknowledge the sincerity of our fellow Christians, who do not see eye to eye with us in such matters, and regard them as inferior Christians? Do we sometimes in quite other matters, where there is no question of right or wrong at issue, interfere in other people's lives out of plain will-to-power?

BUT IF A MAN SUFFER AS A CHRISTIAN, really as a Christian and not for some other reason, LET HIM NOT BE ASHAMED; BUT LET HIM GLORIFY GOD IN THIS NAME. The name 'Christian' occurs three times in the New Testament —in Acts 11.26, 26.28, and here. It was originally a nickname given to members of the Church by those outside, which is proof at least that the first Christians left men no room for doubt about what was the heart of their message. We may perhaps wonder whether 'Christian' would be so obvious a name for some who are called by it to-day! To suffer as a Christian is no matter for shame. If bearing it proudly brings with it suffering, such suffering is a means of glorifying God in this name, And, even though we are not called to suffer as martyrs, we may still glorify God by our bearing the name of Christian. But we are apt to apply it to ourselves very lightly, without asking whether God is really glorified by our association with Christ's name, or whether perhaps our association with it may not often bring Him dishonour.

There follow two verses, whose connection with what has so far been said is on a first reading not immediately clear. FOR THE TIME IS COME FOR JUDGMENT TO BEGIN AT THE HOUSE OF GOD: AND IF IT BEGIN FIRST AT US, WHAT SHALL BE THE END OF THEM THAT OBEY NOT THE GOSPEL OF GOD? AND IF THE RIGHTEOUS IS SCARCELY SAVED, WHERE SHALL THE UNGODLY AND SINNER APPEAR? The connection of thought seems to be that the persecution, which the readers of the letter are suffering, is part of the beginning of the Last Judgment (cf. 'the beginning of travail', Mark 13.8). The last times have begun, though the end is not yet come. The idea that the divine judgment begins at the Church is derived from the Old Testament (e.g. Jer. 25.29, Ezek. 9.6). 'House of God' here means the household of God, God's people, not merely the Temple. The idea of the second half of verse 17 is that the judgment will get more terrible as it goes on. With this we may compare the words of Jesus recorded in Luke 23.31: 'If they do these things in the green tree, what shall be done in the dry?' So to be among the first to be judged is a privilege (there is perhaps the same idea in 1 Cor. 11.32?). But, if the judgment is severe enough even at its beginning, while it is the turn of believers for judgment, it will be far worse for those whose turn will come afterwards, the unbelievers. Peter's motive here, as Beare rightly points out, is not to warn unbelievers, but to encourage believers to endure steadfastly; so the believers are reminded that, terrible though their ordeal is, they are at least facing a less severe ordeal than the disobedient will have to face; at the same time, what is said is a warning that it is no use seeking an escape from the present sufferings of persecution by apostasy, because that would be simply a case of 'out of the frying-pan into the fire'. Verse 18 is a quotation from Proverbs 11.31 (LXX) in confirmation of what has already been said.

The conclusion to all this is: WHEREFORE LET THEM ALSO THAT SUFFER ACCORDING TO THE WILL OF GOD COMMIT THEIR SOULS (or 'themselves') IN WELL-DOING UNTO A FAITHFUL CREATOR. Their sufferings are according to God's will, inasmuch as they are God's judgment beginning at His household, whereby their faith is tested and refined. So they are to commit themselves, trust themselves, into God's hands. The word here rendered 'commit' is the same as that rendered 'commend' in Luke 23.46, and it is likely that the prayer of Christ on the cross was in Peter's mind, a prayer which was not extempore, but came from Ps. 31.5 with one word 'Father' significantly added. Once more Peter bids his readers follow the example of their Lord. This commitment of themselves to God is not to be a matter of passive resignation, but of active well-doing, in love and service. The words 'in well-doing' are in Greek very emphatic, being placed at the end of the sentence. Persecution and suffering are not to be allowed to weaken their efforts; they are not to grow weary of active well-doing. If their trust is real, and they know themselves in God's safe-keeping, they will be enabled to continue in the labour of love. The choice of the word 'Creator' here does not mean that our confidence is to be based on a general belief in God as Creator apart from the revelation in Christ. It is chosen in order to suggest the power which is almighty and therefore able to save and protect. The Good News is precisely that this God, who is Creator and almighty, and who is our Judge, is revealed and active in Jesus Christ His Son. Christ crucified and risen is the proof that God is faithful,[1] and keeps His promises.

[1] Cf. 2 Cor. 1.18, 20, etc.

CHAPTER THIRTEEN

SHEPHERDS OF GOD'S FLOCK
(5.1-4)

THE next four verses are a charge to pastors—THE ELDERS THEREFORE AMONG YOU I EXHORT. . . . The connection in the writer's mind with what precedes is indicated by the word 'therefore'. The fiery trial with its temptations to apostasy, the judgment beginning at the house of God, the challenge to Christians to commit their souls in well-doing to a faithful Creator, as they are called to suffer—these things make all the more urgent the need for faithfulness in pastoral care. The perils of the times are to be an added incentive to the faithful discharge of pastoral duties. The dangers besetting the flock in 1949 are different from those of 63 or 64, but hardly less serious. Seeing that these things are so, what manner of parsons ought ye to be. . . !

But the term: 'elders',[1] though it clearly has an official connotation here (whereas in verse 5 it probably refers simply to age), must not be understood in too definite and limited a sense. It probably includes all those who have some sort of authorized pastoral function and responsibility. So, if we want to hear the message of this passage for to-day, we must realize that, while it has a very special relevance to ordained ministers, its range also includes all who have any pastoral responsibility at all. That means that elders and class-leaders, Sunday School teachers, Church youth club leaders, Bible class leaders, women's meeting sick visitors, and officers of various uniformed

---

[1] For elder cf. Acts 11.30, 14.23, 15.2, 16.4, 20.17, 21.18, 1 Tim. 5.17, Tit. 1.5, Jas. 5.14, etc. Those, who in Acts 20.17 are called ' elders ' are in verse 28 called ' bishops '. Cf. also the more general terms, ' them that are over you in the Lord ' (1 Thess. 5.12), ' he that ruleth ' (Rom. 12.8) ' them that had the rule over you ' (Heb. 13.7).

organizations attached to churches, and certainly those Christians who are school teachers—these all come at once within range. And there are many more, with titles differing according to their various denominations and traditions. 'Elder' may refer to someone very young—for instance, the youngest Sunday School teacher. And even if we hold absolutely no office ecclesiastical, we dare not conclude that what is here said has nothing to do with us!—for there is no communicant who is without a measure of pastoral responsibility for his or her fellows. There is always someone a little weaker, who needs your support and encouragement, someone in danger of wandering, whose feet you can help to keep on the way of life. One thing that is most vitally needed in the renewal of the churches is that we should rediscover the full meaning of pastoral care, not as being only a one-sided responsibility, a burden of the clergy in which the laity have no share, but as including also a reciprocal relationship of all the members of the Church (though this is by no means to deny the special place of the ordained ministry). We have to think out afresh what pastoral care really means, and this passage will help us to do it.

There is a special intimacy about this section. The personality of Peter seems to come forward, though with a notable modesty and restraint. We seem to feel the humility and gentleness of one who once was self-reliant and impetuous, but has been chastened and refined. We may guess that behind these words there lies the memory of the conversation recorded in John 21.15-19. Peter gives a threefold description of himself—WHO AM A FELLOW-ELDER, AND A WITNESS OF THE SUFFERINGS OF CHRIST, WHO AM ALSO A PARTAKER OF THE GLORY THAT SHALL BE REVEALED. It is not his apostolic authority that he here appeals to; rather he chooses—or, it may be, coins—a term, which places him at the side of those he is addressing, as their equal, their 'fellow-elder', who shares with them the pastoral responsibility. The compound word expresses effectively the Apostle's modesty (an avoidance of that self-assertion which was so characteristic of the Simon Peter of the Gospels) and his sympathy and solidarity with those he addresses. He and they are 'in on' the same great task together. The personal poignancy of the second descriptive phrase will easily be realized by referring to the following passages (in this order): Mark 14.29, Luke 22.31f., Mark 14.32-42, 47, John 18.10f., Mark 14.50, 54, 66-72, Luke 22.61, Mark 16.7. How deeply must what he had witnessed have been engraved on his memory! The indelible impression of that uncomplaining Sufferer had broken down his self-reliance and arrogance and transformed his character, and it was the compelling incentive to the care of the flock. The third phrase may refer either to the fact that he had been one of the three, who had been present at Jesus' Transfiguration (Mark 9.2ff.), and on that occasion had experienced a foretaste of the glory that would finally be revealed at His second coming, or else simply to the future glory of the second coming, in which all Christians will share, but in which the Apostles might expect a special place (cf. Matt. 19.28).

The task of the elders is to TEND (or 'shepherd') THE FLOCK OF GOD. Here is a metaphor (cf. 2.25), that has a long history. In the Old Testament human beings are often likened to sheep. Sometimes the point of comparison is the tendency of sheep to stray (e.g. Isa. 53.6, Ps. 119.176), or their helplessness when left to themselves without a shepherd (e.g. Num. 27.17, 1 Kings 22.17). Most frequently it is the people of Israel that is likened to a flock of sheep. While, on the one hand, the metaphor depicts the waywardness and helplessness of the people, it is used, on the other hand, to depict God's care for His people. He is Israel's Shepherd; they are His flock (e.g. Isa. 40.11, Ps. 23, 80.1, 95.7). The Old Testament also speaks of human rulers as shepherds (e.g. Num. 27.17, 2 Sam. 5.2, 7.7, Jer. 12.10, Ezek. 34.1ff.), but it was Israel's tragedy that these human shepherds of hers so often proved unfaithful, feeding themselves instead of feeding the sheep (e.g. Jer. 23.1f., Ezek. 34.1-10, Isa. 56.11, Zech. 11.16f.). God's answer to this unfaithfulness on the part of the human shepherds of His flock is the promise that He will Himself intervene as the true Shepherd of His people (e.g. Ezek. 34.15, Jer. 31.10), and side by side with—or indeed interwoven with—this promise is another promise, that of faithful shepherds to replace the unfaithful (Jer. 23.4), or, as in Ezek. 34.23,

37.24, of a king of David's line, who shall be a faithful shepherd (cf. Mic. 5.2ff.). Thus the metaphor had a definitely Messianic association. We also hear in Zech. 13.7 of a faithful shepherd, who will be smitten, so that the sheep will be scattered.

Jesus takes up this metaphor, which is so rich in associations. He Himself is the Good Shepherd, who is faithful and no hireling. See the following: Matt. 18.12-14 = Luke 15.4-7, Matt. 9.36, 10.6, Mark 6.34, Luke 12.32, 19.10, John 10.1-18. In Him both the promise that God Himself will intervene as Shepherd and the promise of the king-shepherd of David's line are fulfilled. He has come to seek the lost and gather the scattered, and He addresses His disciples as 'little flock', as being the nucleus of the redeemed Israel of God. In John 21.15-19 and in Acts 20.28f., as in this passage of 1 Peter, men are commissioned to be under-shepherds under Christ in the care of His flock. The former passage is particularly significant for us.

The chief functions of the shepherd, as they are depicted in the Bible, are to seek out the lost, gather the scattered, watch over and defend against wild beasts and robbers, to feed and water, to lead. All these Christ the Good Shepherd fulfils Himself, and we are bidden to allow Him to be our Shepherd. But those who themselves experience His shepherding are called in their turn to the work of under-shepherds, helpers of the Good Shepherd in the care of the flock. This pastoral responsibility of the under-shepherds can only be rightly understood in relation to Christ's pastoral responsibility as the 'Chief Shepherd' (verse 4). It is a sharing in His work, and our shepherding is altogether dependent upon His.

The flock the elders are charged to tend is called 'the flock of God'. It is God's, not theirs, nor ours. The Church is always God's possession, not men's. A church that could be ours would be only a false church. So the sheep are not ours for us to use or misuse as we like. If we lose one, we lose Another's property, not our own; and He is not indifferent to what becomes of His flock. The words, 'of God', are both solemn and cheering—solemn, in that they remind us of our responsibility to Him, cheering in their assurance that He will not forsake His own.

The phrase, WHICH IS AMONG YOU, denotes that part of the flock committed to a particular elder's care. To each one of us is entrusted one bit of God's precious flock. It may be a parish or a Sunday School class, or one's workmates, one's own family, or a single friend. Whether it is small or large, the important thing is that a man should see it as the part of God's flock committed to his care, as one of Christ's under-shepherds.

At this point the R.V. has the words EXERCISING THE OVERSIGHT; but, as the Greek word *episkopountes,* which they represent, is omitted by two of the most important manuscripts, it is probable that they should be omitted. At all events, they do not really add anything that is not already included in the meaning of 'tend'.

There follows a series of three pairs of adverbs or adverbial phrases, in which Peter says some very searching things about what are the wrong, and what are the right, spirit and motives, with which to undertake and fulfil pastoral responsibilities. In each pair he sets forth first what is to be avoided, and then that which is to be aimed at. The first pair is: NOT OF CONSTRAINT, BUT WILLINGLY, ACCORDING UNTO GOD. There are different kinds of constraint —some good and some bad. The good sort of constraint, to which Peter is not referring, is mentioned, for instance, in 1 Cor. 9.16, where Paul says, 'Necessity (same Greek root as "constraint" here) is laid upon me; for woe is unto me, if I preach not the gospel.' That is a divine constraint. When this sort of constraint is lacking in a preacher, there is something wrong. Moreover, a certain reluctance to undertake pastoral responsibility may be a good thing, showing a right humility and a realization of the importance of what is to be undertaken, while a too easy readiness might well indicate a glib underestimation of the work and a conceited overestimation of one's own fitness. But there are other kinds of constraint that are unworthy—and it is to these that the Apostle is referring here. For instance, the reluctance, which may make constraint necessary, may be due to the fear of danger (in times of persecution to be a leader is to run a greater risk), and it is unworthy to hold back from responsibility for fear of danger—or, for that matter, just out of disinclination for the hard, and sometimes discouraging, work involved. Another sort of constraint that is to be avoided is social pressure of the kind referred to in 2 Cor. 9.7, Philem. 14. This sort of social pressure can easily force a man into the ministry (e.g. when everybody assumes that the minister's son will follow his father) and the same sort of thing can happen with other forms of pastoral responsibility.

The positive member of this first pair of contrasts is 'willingly, according unto God'. God loves a cheerful giver. The meaning of this phrase is best seen in the whole-heartedness of the Chief Shepherd Himself, who could say, 'My meat is to do the will of him that sent me, and to accomplish his work.'

The second pair of contrasts is: NOR YET FOR FILTHY LUCRE, BUT OF A READY MIND. 'For filthy lucre' represents a Greek adverb compounded of an adjective meaning 'shameful' and a noun meaning 'gain'. 'Lucre' of course includes financial gain, but it includes also much more than that. As far as financial gain is concerned, what Peter says is not an objection to the principle of a paid ministry, nor does it forbid pastors to want a living wage, but it is a warning against covetousness, against all sordid preoccupation with material advantages. But there are other forms of 'gain', that are probably a far greater source of temptation than money. For instance, there is the desire for personal popularity and for making a name. The danger here is all the more to be feared, because it is so very easy to deceive oneself completely. How easy it is for a minister to build up his congregation around his own personality, instead of around the Lord of the Church, and not know that he is doing it, and, while he thinks that he is spending himself sacrificially for the sake of Christ, all the time to be seeking a personal following far more than to make followers of His Lord. And which of us is quite free from such self-seeking? How often is the man, who feels most free from it, the one who is most completely immersed in it? Here is a pit, from which every minister needs to pray constantly that he may be delivered.

Contrasted with 'for filthy lucre' is 'of a ready mind' —or better 'zealously', 'eagerly'. They are not to have the spirit of hirelings, who have to be bribed by the lure of some sordid gain; but they are to do their work for love of the Good Shepherd and His flock, not for some temporal advantage, but because it is their joy to serve their Lord.

The third danger, that Peter warns us against, is that of being corrupted by power—NEITHER AS LORDING IT OVER THE CHARGE ALLOTTED TO YOU. The will-to-power motive belongs to the world, it should have no place in the Church. 'They which are accounted to rule over the Gentiles lord it over (same word as here) them . . . but it is not so among you,' Jesus had said (Mark 10.41-45; cf. 9.33-37). But how extensively does the worldly view of power penetrate and permeate the life of the Church! The truth of the saying that 'power corrupts' is far too often confirmed in the Church, and when spiritual leadership is abused in this way, 'the corruption of the best is worst!' The temptation for the clergy is greatest; but it is by no means limited to them. Again, the danger is all the more formidable, because we are all so good at self-deceit. Once more, the Apostle draws our attention to an abyss of corruption at our very feet.

It is worth lingering a moment over the phrase 'the charge allotted to you'. In the Greek it is simply the definite article with the plural of *kleros*, which in classical Greek means (1) a lot, (2) a portion of land assigned by the civic authorities to a citizen, usually by lot, an allotment. Here used in the plural it must refer to the portions of the one flock that are committed to the care of the several pastors. But to those who were familiar with the LXX, a further thought would be suggested. In the LXX *kleros* was closely associated with *kleronomia,* and, like it, was used to translate the Hebrew *nachalah*—'inheritance' (cf. p. 24). It was used of Canaan as the inheritance given by God to Israel; it was also used of Israel as God's inheritance. It is quite probable that the Apostle has this association in mind here, so that he means 'the parts of God's inheritance (i.e. the Church, the true Israel) which are entrusted to you'. That is why the A.V. has here 'God's heritage'; but the A.V. rendering fails to bring out the significance of the plural. The phrase 'the flock of God which is among you' in the previous verse would suggest that here too the right rendering will be the one that expresses both ideas—both

H

the idea of the inheritance belonging to God and that of its being portioned out in trust to the different pastors.

The positive part of this last pair of contrasts is: BUT MAKING YOURSELVES ENSAMPLES TO THE FLOCK. Instead of using their position of pastoral responsibility as a means to the satisfaction of their instinctive lust for power, let them study so to imitate the humility and unselfishness of Christ, that each of them may be able to say without too colossal incongruity, 'Be ye imitators of me, even as I also am of Christ.'

There follows the promise: AND WHEN THE CHIEF SHEPHERD SHALL BE MANIFESTED, YE SHALL RECEIVE THE CROWN OF GLORY THAT FADETH NOT AWAY. The picture of the crown as the reward of faithful Christians occurs elsewhere in the New Testament (1 Cor. 9.25, 2 Tim. 4.8, Jas. 1.12, Rev. 2.10, 3.11, 4.4); several times it is, as here, associated with Christ's coming in glory. The crown that the New Testament writers had in mind was not the emblem of royalty, but rather the garland or wreath which was the reward for victory in the great Greek athletic festivals. Those who faithfully fulfil the office of under-shepherd, will receive their prize when their Master, the Chief Shepherd, comes in His glory. Their glory, like His, will be, not the glory of this earth that passes away, but the glory of God that abides for ever; and their crowns, unlike the garlands of the Olympic victors, will never fade or wither.

CHAPTER FOURTEEN

FINAL EXHORTATIONS

(5.5-11)

THE use of the word 'elder' in its technical sense in the last section apparently suggested—not unnaturally—the thought of its primary meaning, and so in verse 5 the Apostle goes on to say something about the relation between young and old. LIKEWISE (the word is used here simply to make the transition to another matter), YE YOUNGER, BE SUBJECT UNTO THE ELDER. For the meaning of 'be subject' see Chapter VI. As in the case of the slaves and their masters, Peter only deals directly with one side, the humbler side, of the relationship. Instead of going on to bid the older people fulfil their obligations towards the younger he follows his word to the younger by a general exhortation to all to serve one another, which of course includes the other. Perhaps he was influenced by the fact that he had already addressed a section to the 'elders' in the technical sense. Lest anyone should leap to the conclusion that the New Testament provides a charter for every sort of conservatism and a sanction for the domestic tyrant type of parent, or that it approves of such notions as that the young are to be seen and not heard, and that any criticism on the part of the young is to be summarily suppressed, it is perhaps as well to point out that the New Testament does also speak of the duty of parents to their children (Eph. 6.4) and that the young Timothy is warned against allowing his flock to presume upon his youthfulness (1 Tim. 4.12)!

Friction between the generations is a perennial problem; but in recent years it has been aggravated by a number of causes. The lengthening of the average span of life by the advance of science coinciding with a decrease in the size of families has resulted in an increase of the relative number of aged people in the community, who have to be supported by fewer workers. The destruction of life in two world wars has further reduced the numbers in the middle age-groups in comparison with the young and the old. The relative scarcity of the young and the urgent economic need for them as workers have caused much greater attention to be paid to them than in the past. The fashion of the age, according to which youth is all-important, though largely the creation of economic and strategic needs, has been widely reflected in the churches. This change of outlook in the churches, we may suspect, is less the result of deepening understanding of the Gospel and more the result of the change of fashion in the world than is generally supposed. But the tendency to ' over-fuss ' the young is liable to aggravate their natural self-assertiveness, and still further to increase the rift between the generations. It would therefore seem that Peter's exhortation to the younger is of special importance for to-day. It reminds those who are particularly liable to be taken up completely with their own rights of their obligations to others. It bids them set bounds to their instinctive self-assertiveness—at a time when self-expression is a popular catch-word. On the other hand, it claims respect and courtesy for those who, in these materialistic days, are an economic liability on the community.

But what would doubtless be more in Peter's mind is the need to learn discipline in one's youth and to profit by the experience of others, and a real concern for order. The Gospel was indeed revolutionary and Christians were turning the world upside down (Acts 17.6); but it was not revolution in the interests of chaos and disorder, but on the contrary an attack on the established disorder of the world in the interests and in the strength of divine order. So there was nothing Christian in throwing all common sense to the winds, and Peter might be expected to remind any of the younger element in the Church, who were tempted to imagine that they knew all the answers and had no need to learn from others, that their self-confidence was no Christian virtue. We may also perhaps without being too fanciful hear in this word to the ' younger ' another message; for in a sense the whole Church militant is young in relation to the Church triumphant, and just as the young are liable to think they can do without the experience of their elders, so too the Church of to-day is sometimes liable to think that it need not stop to consider the experience of Church history. Perhaps that is a special danger of the younger denominations.

From the relation of old and young Peter goes on to a general exhortation addressed to all alike: YEA, ALL OF YOU GIRD YOURSELVES WITH HUMILITY, TO SERVE ONE ANOTHER. We have already heard about humility in 3.8. The word translated 'gird' is a curious one; it means 'to tie on securely', and it is probable that the substantive formed from it referred specially to the apron worn by slaves. It seems likely that Peter has in mind the memorable occasion when Jesus had girded Himself with a towel to wash His disciples' feet (John 13.1-15). We may also compare Mark 10.45, Luke 22.27. As the Lord Jesus Himself was content to be among men as one that serves, so His disciples must follow the pattern of His humility, and be ready to serve one another. 'If I then, the Lord and the Master, have washed your feet, ye also ought to wash one another's feet.'

Peter adds a reason: FOR GOD RESISTETH THE PROUD, BUT GIVETH GRACE TO THE HUMBLE. It is a quotation from Proverbs 3.34 (LXX). The proud man has God for his Adversary (cf. Num. 22.22ff.), but to the humble God shows favour.

The letter goes on: HUMBLE YOURSELVES THEREFORE UNDER THE MIGHTY HAND OF GOD, THAT HE MAY EXALT YOU IN DUE TIME. The mighty hand of God is a figure which occurs frequently in the Old Testament (e.g. Exod. 13.9, Deut. 3.24, 9.26), for God's mighty intervention in human affairs in judgment and mercy. We are to recognize God's hand not only in the joys that come to us, but also in the sorrows and afflictions that humble us (in view of 4.12-19, doubtless Peter was thinking particularly of persecution). Of course, human sin is an ingredient in most of our trials, but God can make even the wrath of men to praise Him (Ps. 76.10), and He turns what men mean for evil to our true advantage. Two verses in Genesis are specially suggestive in this connection (Gen. 45.8 and 50.20). In the one place Joseph says: 'So now it was not you that sent me hither, but God'; and in the other: 'As for you, ye meant evil against me; but God meant it for good'. We may compare some words from the Heidelberg Catechism (1563), which will bear pondering. 'In Him (i.e. God the Father) I trust, and doubt not, but that He will care for me . . . and that even all the troubles, which He sends to me in this vale of tears, He will turn to my good. This as almighty God He can do, and as my faithful Father He will do . . . health and sickness, riches and poverty, are not works of chance; but these all come to us from His fatherly hand' (Questions 26f.). So we are not to fret and chafe under affliction, but to know that we are in God's hand. We are to accept those afflictions, which like persecution most obviously come by the sin of others, not in a spirit of resentment, as seeing only the spite and cruelty of men, but we are to recognize rather the permitting hand of God, who loves us, and so endure humbly and patiently. Our humiliation will not last for ever; for those, whom God now allows to share the humiliations of His Son's earthly life, He will presently cause to share His Son's glory. The words 'in due time' point to the coming again of Christ.

To recognize the fatherly hand of God is to be released from anxiety: CASTING ALL YOUR ANXIETY UPON HIM, BECAUSE HE CARETH FOR YOU. The actual form of expression of the first half of this comes from Ps. 55.22, where the LXX has 'Cast upon the Lord thy anxiety'; but no doubt the memory of Christ's teaching was in Peter's mind. In Matt. 6.25-34 there is the same emphasis on the fact that God cares for us, and therefore we need not be anxious. We may also compare Phil. 4.6. The Christian is invited to let God carry the burden of his anxiety. If we are sufficiently humble to be willing to do it, we may cast our worry upon Him. Whether we do it or not is a test of the sincerity and reality of our humbleness.

'He careth for you' sums up the heart of the Gospel. God is not indifferent to our troubles; we are His concern. Sometimes it is desperately hard for us to believe it. At such times all lesser arguments and would-be proofs of the goodness of God are liable to appear ambiguous, and to urge them is to mock us. The one solid argument is the cross of Christ and His resurrection. Golgotha is both the demonstration and the measure of God's caring.

BE SOBER is an exhortation that we have already had

twice in the course of the letter (1.13, 4.7). BE WATCHFUL (or 'watch') is a word that must have had very poignant associations for Peter. At the end of the conversation about 'the last things' recorded in Mark 13 Jesus had warned His disciples to watch. A little later, when He warned them of His approaching sufferings, Peter had boasted 'Although all shall be offended (caused to stumble), yet will not I', and 'If I must die with thee, I will not deny thee'. Then in Gethsemane Jesus had said to the three disciples, 'My soul is exceeding sorrowful even unto death: abide ye here and watch'. But they had slept, and Peter had been one of them. 'And he cometh, and findeth them sleeping, and saith unto Peter, Simon, sleepest thou? couldest thou not watch one hour? Watch and pray, that ye enter not into temptation. . . .' Three times Jesus had come and found them sleeping. Jesus had bidden Peter watch, and he had slept. He had bidden him be on the watch against temptation, and Peter had been caught off his guard by the maid-servant, and denied his Lord. And now the disciple, who had himself on more than one occasion failed to watch, but who had been restored by his Lord, bids his readers 'Watch'.

And how necessary are sobriety and watchfulness!—for YOUR ADVERSARY THE DEVIL, AS A ROARING LION, WALKETH ABOUT, SEEKING WHOM HE MAY DEVOUR. It was that same devil, about whom Jesus had warned Peter, 'Simon, Simon, behold Satan asked to have you, that he might sift you as wheat' (Luke 22.31), and he is still ever on the move, going hither and thither, never resting in his efforts to find those whom he can devour. He has many disguises, and is no less dangerous when his approach is most friendly and plausible. Here Peter is probably thinking mainly of persecution with its temptations to apostasy. The simile of the lion was perhaps suggested by the lions in the arena, or perhaps more probably by Ps. 22.13. The only right reaction to the devil, in whatever disguise he may appear, is to resist him: WHOM WITHSTAND STEDFAST IN YOUR FAITH. What is called for is no superficial or sentimental faith, but a faith that is strong and immovable, like a great rock. And you will be helped to stand firm by KNOWING THAT THE SAME SUFFERINGS ARE being ACCOMPLISHED IN YOUR BRETHREN

WHO ARE IN THE WORLD. Those who have belonged to a
'Church under the cross', have often found comfort and
strength in the knowledge that they were not suffering alone,
but that brothers and sisters elsewhere were suffering in the
same cause—and suffering bravely.

But that is not all. The Christian message is not just
exhortation to resist, to watch, to be sober, etc. If that were
all and if everything depended on us, on our resistance and
watchfulness and sobriety, it would indeed be a poor pros-
pect for us. But Christian exhortation is always set in the
context of the Gospel. So here Peter goes on to the
promise: AND THE GOD OF ALL GRACE (i.e. the God, whose
nature is altogether gracious and whose dealings with us are
altogether grace), WHO CALLED YOU UNTO HIS ETERNAL
GLORY IN CHRIST, AFTER THAT YE HAVE SUFFERED A LITTLE
WHILE (cf. 1.6), SHALL HIMSELF PERFECT, STABLISH,
STRENGTHEN YOU. The word 'himself' is emphatic. Ultimately our salvation is altogether His work. Our hope
stands not in our own strength and loyalty to Him, but in
His strength and His faithfulness, not in our hold on Him,
but in His hold on us. We may compare Phil. 1.6, 1 Thess.
5.24.

The word translated 'shall perfect' is interesting. The
same word is used in Mark 1.19 of fishermen mending nets.
It was also used of repairing and recommissioning a dam-
aged ship. God will Himself renew their strength and repair
the damage done by their sufferings and by their falterings
and stumblings and make them fit for further service.

Peter closes his last exhortations with a doxology: TO
HIM BE THE DOMINION FOR EVER AND EVER. AMEN. A dox-
ology is a fitting conclusion to exhortation that is really
Christian exhortation; because it is not just a matter of
'Try again' and 'Try harder', but is set in the context of
the grace and faithfulness of God.

CHAPTER FIFTEEN

FINAL GREETINGS

(5.12-14)

W E now come to the conclusion of the letter with its final greetings. Paul, who made use of the services of an amanuensis for the actual writing of his letters, appears generally to have written the concluding words with his own hand,[1] and it is probable that Peter similarly would have added these last sentences with his own hand, or at least dictated them verbatim. Silvanus is hardly likely to have composed the commendation of the 'faithful brother' himself. So we may imagine the aged Apostle at this point taking the pen from his friend's hands.

BY SILVANUS, OUR FAITHFUL BROTHER, AS I ACCOUNT HIM, I HAVE WRITTEN UNTO YOU. His reason for commending Silvanus is presumably that he was to be the bearer of the letter, though we need not suppose that he would necessarily visit all the churches mentioned in 1.1 himself—the letter would more probably be copied in Asia Minor, and some of the churches receive copies rather than the original document. The fact that Peter puts 'I have written' rather than 'I have sent' suggests that Silvanus was the amanuensis and not just the bearer. But by itself it gives us no indication how much responsibility the amanuensis had. Such amanuenses were sometimes left very free to compose letters according to the general gist or intention of their principals, while sometimes they merely wrote to dictation. We have already seen reason to believe that Silvanus had a real share in the actual composition of the letter. The definite article in the Greek before 'faithful brother', which the R.V. renders by 'our', perhaps indicates that he was already well known to those who were to receive the letter.

In commending Silvanus Peter fixes upon the one really

[1] 1 Cor. 16.21, Gal. 6.11, Col. 4.18, 2 Thess. 3.17 (which is particularly interesting), and Philem. 19.

important thing about him—that he is a loyal Christian. That is the significance of 'the faithful brother'. He does not commend him as the eloquent and gifted man that he undoubtedly was, nor for personal charm, but simply as a sincere Christian.

He says that he has written to them BRIEFLY. As a letter this could scarcely be called brief, but in comparison with the greatness of its theme it is (cf. Heb. 13.22).

The character and purpose of the letter are well summed up in the words EXHORTING AND TESTIFYING THAT THIS IS THE TRUE GRACE OF GOD: STAND YE FAST THEREIN (literally, 'wherein stand fast'). Exhortation and testimony—that well describes the letter. The two things are intertwined with each other. Whereas others might—more logically and more neatly maybe—put first testimony and then as a separate division the exhortation that follows from it, Peter's way is to weave the two strands together: testimony—the apostolic witness to the truth as it is in Jesus, the doctrinal strand of the letter; and exhortation—the appeal by that truth and in view of it to walk worthy of it. The two strands are woven together once more in this summing-up sentence: testimony to the truth of that Gospel by which his readers live, the reality of the grace in which they stand, and, on the other hand, exhortation to them steadfastly to abide in it. Some of the Greek manuscripts have the indicative, 'wherein ye stand', but the better ones have the imperative, 'wherein stand'. The imperative is probably the correct reading. Peter has tried to say two things at once, and he has telescoped the two together. He wants to say: 'The grace in which you stand is the true grace of God' and at the same time he wants to exhort them to go on standing fast in it. So in the relative clause he substitutes an imperative for the indicative, thus running the two thoughts together. He is saying to them—and to us—You need have no fear lest the Gospel might prove to be false; your faith in Christ is faith in the living God; what you have to do with in Jesus Christ is truly God's grace, God's love in action; in trusting in Him you have not put your trust in a mere man, nor in any of the changing ideologies or idealisms of men, nor in any human wishful thinking or day-dreaming, but in the eternal, unchanging God. There is no question about the truth of the Gospel of Jesus Christ, but only about the reality and depth of your understanding of it and the firmness with which you trust in it. Therefore abide in it, cleave to it, let your roots go down ever deeper and deeper into it.

Now the actual greetings begin: SHE THAT IS IN BABYLON, ELECT TOGETHER WITH YOU, SALUTETH (greeteth) YOU. It is improbable that the reference is to Peter's wife; rather it is to the local church. There is no difficulty in understanding the feminine substantive *ekklesia* ('church'). 'Babylon' here is neither the ancient city in Mesopotamia, nor the Roman garrison-town in Egypt, but stands for Rome (cf. Rev. 17., 18). Behind its use here there is no doubt the conviction that the capital of the Empire is the contemporary Babylon, the proud mistress of the nations and the centre of worldly and pagan power—and perhaps also prudential reasons for not mentioning Rome.

The church in Rome is 'elect together with' those scattered churches away in Asia Minor, to which the letter is addressed. They are bound together, because they are objects of the same gracious divine action. *Syneklektos* ('elect together with') is a word upon which we may well ponder in connection with our problems of reunion. It should help us in distinguishing the cart from the horse!

One individual is singled out as sending his greetings: AND SO DOTH MARK MY SON. We may safely identify this Mark with the writer of the Gospel. His mother's house was apparently the rendezvous of the early Jerusalem Church. Thither Peter had gone after his miraculous release from prison (Acts 12.12), and had found many gathered together praying. It was possibly the scene of the Last Supper and of some of the Resurrection appearances. It is a plausible suggestion that Mark was himself the young man of Mark 14.51f. He was the cousin of Barnabas, and accompanied Paul and Barnabas on part of the First Missionary Journey (Acts 12.25), but left them and returned home (13.13), thus causing an estrangement between Paul and Barnabas (15.37-39). Later Paul forgave him, and we find them together (Col. 4.10f., Philem. 24). It would seem that after Paul's death Mark worked in close association with Peter. An early and reliable tradition associated them together in Rome. Eusebius' quotation from Papias (c. A.D. 140) is well known: 'Mark, having become the interpreter of Peter, wrote down accurately everything that he remembered, without however recording in order what was said or done by Christ.'

Peter next bids his readers SALUTE ONE ANOTHER WITH A KISS OF LOVE. There are similar sentences in Paul's letters (Rom. 16.16, 1 Cor. 16.20, 2 Cor. 13.12, 1 Thess. 5.26). In Justin's time (middle of second century A.D.) the kiss was a regular feature of the Eucharist, coming between the intercessory prayers and the offertory. It was the sign and pledge of unity and charity between the brethren, and great stress was laid on the necessity for those who had a quarrel to be reconciled before participation—'lest your sacrifice be defiled' (Didache 14.2). In the east before the kiss of peace the deacon used to cry aloud from beside the bishop's throne, 'Is there any man that keepeth ought against his fellow?' A century later the deacon's proclamation was, 'Let none keep rancour against any! Let none give the kiss in hypocrisy!' In this connection some of the Fathers cite Matt. 5.23f. It has been pointed out that Judas' choice of the kiss as a sign (Mark 14.44) implies that it was in common use among Jesus' disciples, while Luke 7.45 shows that Jesus valued it as a token of affection. It is not unlikely (though it is not proved) that the kiss was used in the Eucharist from New Testament times, and that it is to this Eucharistic kiss that Peter refers here. (The letter would most probably be read at the Eucharist; for that would be the occasion on which the whole church would be assembled together.) This reference to 'the kiss of love' is one more reminder that unity and love between individual members and between churches are essential to the true being of the Church, one more reminder of the sin and scandal of a divided Church, and of the defectiveness of all our sectarian Eucharists.

The opening greeting of the letter was 'Grace to you and peace be multiplied': the closing greeting is PEACE BE UNTO YOU ALL THAT ARE IN CHRIST. We saw something of the meaning of 'peace' in connection with 1.2. To be 'in Christ' is the condition of receiving it; but it is for 'all' who are in Him without exception.

INDEX

125